INTRODUCTION TO BRRRR REAL ESTATE INVESTING

THE REAL ESTATE INVESTING

MENTOR

THE AFFORDABLE $50K COACHING ALTERNATIVE

James Orr
The Real Estate Financial Planner™

Published by:

Real Estate Financial Planner LLC
PO Box 2163
Loveland CO 80539

https://RealEstateFinancialPlanner.com

First edition November 2024.
File: 2024-11-11 - Introduction to BRRRR Real Estate Investing

This publication is designed to provide accurate and authoritative information regarding the subject matter covered. It is sold with the understanding that the publisher is not engaged in rendering legal, accounting or other professional advice or services. If legal advice or other expert advice is required, the services of a competent professional person should be sought.

From a *Declaration of Principles* jointly adopted by a Committee of American Bar Association and a Committee of Publishers and Associations.

This is a work of fiction. References to clients in this book are fictional and have been modified and changed from any possible real situations to protect the identities of clients and to simplify the stories for clarity. In some cases, significant parts of the stories have been changed. In some cases, stories have been completely fabricated to illustrate a concept. Any similarities to people alive or dead is purely coincidental.

AI Disclosure: While James Orr authored the original version of this content, AI was used extensively to draft, proofread, edit, improve and write subsequent versions and variations.

DEDICATION

Dedicated to my wife Tammy. I have no words.

FREE DOWNLOAD

The World's Greatest Real Estate Deal Analysis Spreadsheet™

Thank you for purchasing this book and taking the next step toward mastering real estate investing.

As a special bonus, you can download *The World's Greatest Real Estate Deal Analysis Spreadsheet*™ for free. This powerful tool will help you analyze deals like a pro, ensuring you make informed, profitable decisions.

Download your free copy now and start running the numbers with confidence.

https://REFP.com/spreadsheet

Table of Contents

ii

Introduction to BRRRR Real Estate Investing

BRRRR is a powerful real estate investing strategy for acquiring properties and leaving little—or ideally nothing—in a deal.

BRRRR is an acronym for Buy, Rehab, Rent, Refinance and (optionally) Repeat.

Let's break down each step of this strategy:

- **Buy** - You start by purchasing a property at a significant discount, typically 70-75% of its After Repair Value (ARV) or lower. This often means looking for distressed or undervalued properties that need work.
- **Rehab** - Next, you renovate the property to increase its value. This step is crucial as it not only improves the property's condition but also its potential rental income and overall value.

- **Rent** - Once the property is in good condition, you rent it out to tenants. This step begins to generate cash flow and demonstrates to lenders that the property is a viable investment.
- **Refinance** - After the property has been rented for a period (usually 6-12 months from the initial purchase for seasoning), you refinance it based on its new, higher value. The goal is to pull out most—or ideally *all*—of your initial investment.
- **Repeat** - With the cash from the refinance, you can now start the process over with a new property, potentially growing your portfolio without investing additional personal funds.

The BRRRR strategy can be a game-changer for your real estate investing journey, but it requires careful planning, market knowledge, and the ability to find great deals.

BRRRR Variations

Let's explore the different variations that can supercharge your real estate portfolio:

- **Traditional BRRRR** - This is the classic approach where you buy a property, renovate it, rent it out for long-term tenants, refinance, and then repeat the process. It's a great way to build a portfolio of cash-flowing properties.
- **BRRRR to Short-Term Rentals** - Instead of long-term tenants, you convert your BRRRR property into a short-term rental. This can potentially yield higher returns.
- **Property Type Variations** - BRRRR isn't limited to single-family homes. You can apply this strategy to duplexes, triplexes, fourplexes, and even small apartment buildings. While less common, you can apply the BRRRR strategy to commercial, industrial, or retail properties.
- **Local vs. Remote BRRRR** - You're not limited to your local market because you're not typically moving into the properties like you would with house hacking or the Nomad™ real estate investing strategies. BRRRR allows you to invest in properties across the country, opening opportunities in markets with better deals, more plentiful deals and/or higher potential returns.

Financing BRRRR

Let's look at some of the more common ways to financing BRRRR deals as well as some of the less common, more unusual ways to finance BRRRR deals.

Remember, with BRRRR we're often financing the property twice: first to acquire the property where we can add value and then, after we've added value, refinancing it to leave as little money in the deal as practically possible—and ideally no money in the deal at all.

Most Common Financing

Here are the most common methods of financing BRRRR properties:

- **Hard Money Loans** - These are short-term loans often used for initial purchase and rehab. They're great for quick closings but come with higher interest rates. You'll typically use hard money loans for the "Buy" and "Rehab" stages. With *BRRRR to Short-Term Rentals*, you might need a larger loan to cover furnishing costs.
- **Private Money** - Hard money loans are from lenders who are in the business of making loans; private money loans are from friends and family not in the business of making loans. Terms can be more flexible, which is helpful if you're BRRRRing and need additional flexibility. You might use private money for the initial purchase, rehab, and furnishing the property if you're converting it to a short-term rental.
- **Traditional Non-Owner-Occupant Loans** - These are typically used for the refinance stage. You'll likely need to wait 6-12 months after purchase (often called seasoning) before refinancing unless you find a lender with a special program that caters to BRRRR investors.

- **Cash** - If you have the funds, buying with cash can give you an edge in competitive markets. This works for all BRRRR variations and property types. After rehab and establishing rental income, you can do a cash-out refinance to recoup your investment.

While financing twice in BRRRR deals can help you leave little money in the deal, it's important to note that this approach does come with significant costs that can eat into your equity.

The expenses associated with two rounds of financing, including closing costs and potentially higher interest rates, can impact your overall returns.

However, BRRRR isn't the only strategy for acquiring rental properties with minimal upfront investment. You might also consider house hacking, the Nomad™ strategy (including a variation that provides unlimited downpayments for subsequent purchases), or various creative financing strategies. These alternatives can help you build your real estate portfolio while minimizing your initial cash outlay, each with its own unique advantages and considerations.

Check out *Introduction to House Hacking Real Estate Investing*, *Introduction to Nomad™ Real Estate Investing*, and *Introduction to Creative Financing* all separate titles in *The Real Estate Investing Mentor* series for more information about other real estate investing strategies that allow you to invest with little or no money.

More Unusual Methods

Let's explore a few of the less common, more unusual methods of financing BRRRR properties:

- **Owner Financing** - In this scenario, the property seller becomes the lender. You make payments directly to them rather than a bank. This approach is particularly useful for BRRRR deals involving properties that might not qualify for traditional financing due to their condition. Depending on how you structure the owner financing, you have two options: leave the owner financing in place (which technically isn't BRRRR since you're not refinancing), or refinance into more permanent, long-term traditional financing after completing repairs and securing tenants. This method works for various property types, from single-family homes to small apartment buildings. Utilizing owner financing during the rehab and rent period can save you from getting an expensive hard money loan.

- **Subject-To Financing** - This method involves taking over the seller's existing mortgage payments without formally assuming the loan. It allows you to acquire the property without qualifying for a new loan. Like owner financing, you have two options: keep the seller's existing financing (which isn't technically BRRRR since you're not refinancing) or refinance the property after completing repairs and securing tenants. If you choose to refinance, you'd typically use long-term, traditional financing. This approach—like owner financing—can potentially save you from resorting to an expensive hard money loan.

- **Wrap Financing** - This creative financing method involves "wrapping" a new loan around the seller's existing mortgage. It's like subject-to financing, but with a key difference: the seller retains the right to foreclose if you default on payments. You pay the seller, who then continues to pay their original mortgage. You may also negotiate additional payments beyond their existing loan to the seller. This approach offers flexibility similar to subject-to financing, potentially helping you avoid expensive hard money loans during the initial stages of your BRRRR project.

Remember, these creative financing methods can be applied to various BRRRR scenarios, whether you're focusing on long-term rentals or short-term vacation properties. They can also be useful when investing in different property types or exploring remote markets where traditional financing might be challenging to secure.

Holding

Let's talk about holding BRRRR properties.

First, how active or passive is investing in BRRRR properties? And then, how long do you typically hold BRRRR properties?

Active/Passive

When it comes to BRRRR investing, you're looking at a strategy that's more on the active side of the real estate investing spectrum.

Here's why:

- **Initial Intensity** - The early stages of BRRRR are particularly hands-on. You're actively involved in finding a property that is both a candidate for adding value and would also make a great rental then you're managing the rehab process and navigating the refinancing phase.
- **Transition to Passive** - Once you've completed the initial stages and secured long-term financing, your BRRRR property starts to resemble a traditional buy-and-hold investment or a short-term rental, depending on your chosen path.
- **Ongoing Management** - Even after the transition, you'll need to actively manage the property or oversee a property management company, especially if you've opted for the short-term rental route.

Duration

When it comes to BRRRR properties, the holding period is typically quite long. In theory, you could hold onto these properties indefinitely, treating them as long-term investments in your real estate portfolio.

However, the reality is often more nuanced.

Here's what you need to know about holding periods for BRRRR properties:

- **Long-Term Investment** - Many investors plan to hold BRRRR properties for extended periods, often 10 years or more. This allows you to benefit from long-term appreciation and ongoing rental income.
- **Leveraging Equity** - Some savvy BRRRR investors choose to leverage the equity they've built up in their properties. You might refinance or take out a home equity loan to fund the purchase of additional properties, potentially accelerating your portfolio growth.
- **Portfolio Simplification** - As you approach retirement, you might decide to simplify your real estate holdings. This could involve selling some of your BRRRR properties to focus on a smaller number of high-performing assets.
- **Transitioning Strategies** - In some cases, you might choose to exit the BRRRR strategy entirely. This could mean selling all your properties to invest in more passive real estate options or diversifying into other investment vehicles.

You might find yourself regularly evaluating whether to hold onto the property or sell it to reinvest the equity you've built. This decision is more common with BRRRR properties where you've captured forced appreciation through the rehab. It's especially relevant since BRRRR properties aren't always ideal long-term rentals; sometimes you buy them simply because you can acquire them and leave little money in the deal after refinancing. If you were choosing a property exclusively for long-term rental potential, you might not have selected this particular property.

Because of this BRRRR investors find themselves considering selling their BRRRR properties and re-allocating their capital into more ideal long-term rentals slightly more than those buying properties solely based on their rental characteristics to begin with.

Exit

In theory you'd hold onto your BRRRR properties forever and utilize their cash flow to achieve financial independence. But the reality is more nuanced and you might find yourself wanting to sell the properties as we previously discuss.

If you were to sell your BRRRR properties, what are the most common channels for selling them? And how will your buyers typically finance the purchases?

Exit Channels

Let's explore your options if you decide to part ways with your BRRRR property:

- **Multiple Listing Service (MLS)** - This is your go-to option for maximum exposure. By listing your property on the MLS, you're tapping into a vast network of real estate agents and potential buyers.
- **For Sale By Owner (FSBO)** - If you're feeling confident in your sales skills, you might consider the FSBO route. This approach can save you money on real

estate agent commissions, but remember, it requires more time and effort on your part. You'll be responsible for marketing, showing the property, and negotiating deals.

- **Auction** - While less common for individual BRRRR properties, auctions can be an effective way to sell quickly. They create a sense of urgency among buyers and can sometimes result in higher prices due to competitive bidding. However, they also come with the risk of selling below market value if bidding is low.

While not a marketing channel itself, utilizing a 1031 tax deferred exchange allows you to defer capital gains taxes and depreciation recapture taxes by reinvesting the proceeds into another "like-kind" property. This is especially true with BRRRR since you're adding some forced appreciation which leads to increased capital gains. Using a 1031 tax deferred exchange can be a great way to upgrade your portfolio without a hefty tax bill.

Check out *Should I Sell My Rental Property?* and *Should I Refinance My Rental Property?* in *The Real Estate Investing Mentor* series for more information on the calculations, considerations and spreadsheets for selling or refinancing your rental properties.

Exit Financing

Next, let's explore the most common financing methods your potential buyers might use:

- **Never Sell** - Many successful BRRRR investors choose to hold onto their properties indefinitely. This approach allows you to benefit from long-term appreciation and ongoing rental income.
- **Traditional Owner-Occupant Loans** - If you're selling to someone who plans to live in the property, they might use conventional mortgages, FHA loans, or VA loans. These often come with lower down payments and better terms for the buyer.
- **Traditional Non-Owner-Occupant Loans** - When selling to another investor, they'll likely use these loans. They typically require a 20-25% down payment and have slightly higher interest rates than owner-occupant loans. Although there are 15% down non-owner-occupant investor loan options with Private Mortgage Insurance (PMI).
- **Cash** - Some buyers, especially experienced investors, might offer cash. This can lead to a faster, smoother closing process, which could be advantageous for you as the seller.

Investor/Entrepreneur

When it comes to real estate investing, you'll find that strategies fall on a spectrum between Real Estate Investing and Real Estate Entrepreneurial approaches. Let's break this down:

Real Estate Investing typically involves primarily putting your money to work. You're looking for a return on your financial investment, often with minimal time commitment.

Think of buying a property and hiring a property manager to handle day-to-day operations.

On the other hand, Real Estate Entrepreneurial strategies require a significant investment of your time, along with some money. Here, you're aiming for a return on both your time and financial investment.

BRRRR is a prime example of a Real Estate Entrepreneurial strategy investing both significant time and money, especially in its early stages.

Here's why:

- **Time Investment** - You'll spend considerable time finding undervalued properties that would also make great rentals, overseeing renovations, and securing tenants.
- **Double Financing** - You'll navigate two rounds of financing: initial purchase and post-renovation refinancing. This requires time, effort, and knowledge of financing programs.
- **Sweat Equity** - Your time and effort in the rehab process directly contribute to increasing the property's value.
- **Active Management** - During the renovation and initial rental period, you'll likely be hands-on with property management.

The goal of BRRRR investors is to convert their time and effort into captured equity. By forcing appreciation through renovations and refinancing, you're essentially creating value with your entrepreneurial efforts.

Remember, while BRRRR starts out highly entrepreneurial, it can transition to a more passive Real Estate Investing approach once you've stabilized the property and potentially hired a property manager.

Money Required

How much money is required to utilize the BRRRR strategy and what do you typically use it for? And, what are some of the less common, more unusual uses of money when BRRRRing?

Most Common

Let's break down the most common money requirements:

- **Little or Nothing Down with Hard Money/Private Money** - This is often your ticket to entry. Hard money or private money lenders can finance your initial purchase and rehab costs, allowing you to get started with minimal cash out of pocket. In an ideal world, you'd leave no money in the deal. However, it is more common to leave something in the deal—often 5-10% of the value of the property.
- **Rehab Costs** - This is where you create value. Your rehab budget covers everything from major renovations to minor cosmetic updates. These costs may be financed initially with hard money loans or private money loans and then refinanced out later. Or, you may choose to fund the rehab costs with your own cash or credit.

- **Closing Costs** - You'll likely face closing costs twice: once for your initial purchase and again when you refinance. These can include appraisal fees, title insurance, and lender fees. Budget for about 2-5% of the loan amount for each transaction but these can vary widely from market to market and lender to lender.
- **Rent Ready Costs** - In addition to your rehab costs, there may be additional things to prepare the property for rent. If you're going to BRRRR into a short-term rental this might include furnishing the property.
- **Cumulative Negative Cash Flow** - This is a crucial consideration in BRRRR investing. You might experience negative cash flow initially, especially if you're using higher-interest hard money loans. Although, I am also explicitly referring to any negative cash flow you might have after you refinance into long-term financing as well. Set aside the total, cumulative amount of negative cash you're likely to see until rents rise enough and cash flow is positive. Here's why:

  o Negative cash flow is really deferred down payment. If you put more down, you wouldn't have negative cash flow. Since you're often trying to minimize the amount you put down with BRRRR properties there is an increased chance of having negative cash flow (also known as deferred down payment).
  o The interest rates on hard money loans while you're rehabbing and waiting to refinance into better interest rate, long-term financing make it more difficult to positive cash flow until after you're refinanced.

- Finding deals that are both discounted and ideal rentals can be challenging. Finding properties to buy at a discount to fix up can be challenging. Adding in that they must also be a great rental once their fixed up, narrows the number of properties that could be used for BRRRR. Often the properties you can buy at a deep discount aren't ideal for long-term rentals and optimized for cash flowing. This increases the chance you'll see some negative cash flow.
- While buying at a discount and rehabbing helps, remember that refinance interest rates are often higher than purchase money mortgages. With strategies like buy and hold, house hacking, and Nomading™, you can often be more selective and find better cash flow deals from the start. And, buy them with slightly better purchase money mortgage interest rates as well.
- Keep in mind, there are exceptions to this. Every market and deal is unique.

- **Reserves** - Set aside money for unexpected repairs, vacancies, or market downturns. A good rule of thumb is to have at least 6 months of all expenses saved as reserves for each property.

Less Common

Let's explore a few of the less common money requirements when utilizing BRRRR:

- **All-Cash Purchase** - If you have the funds available, buying a property outright can give you a significant advantage in competitive markets. After completing the rehab and establishing rental income, you can do a cash-out refinance to recoup your investment. This will also help with cash flow before your refinance compared to higher interest rate hard money loans.
- **Larger Down Payment** - While the BRRRR strategy typically aims to minimize your initial investment, putting more money down upfront can sometimes lead to better loan terms and lower interest rates. This approach might be beneficial if you're looking to maximize cash flow from the start.
- **100% Financing with Hard Money or Private Money** - Some hard money lenders or private investors might be willing to finance the entire purchase price and renovation costs. While this can be an attractive option for investors with limited capital, be prepared for higher interest rates and shorter loan terms.

The ideal scenario in BRRRR investing for many investors is to leave no money in the deal after refinancing. However, in many real estate markets, it's more realistic to expect to leave about 5% to 10% of the property's value in the deal. This still allows for significant leverage and the potential for strong returns on your investment.

Credit Required

When it comes to credit requirements for the BRRRR strategy, you're looking at a two-stage process: the initial purchase and then the refinance.

For the initial purchase, you can often secure a hard money loan. These lenders are often more concerned with the property's potential than your credit score. However, many hard money lenders will still look at you and your credit as the borrower.

The real credit requirement often comes during the refinance stage. This is where you'll typically need to qualify for traditional non-owner-occupant financing.

Here's what you need to know:

- **Credit Score Requirement** - The magic number is usually around 620. This is the typical minimum score lenders look for when considering you for a refinance.
- **Exceptions Exist** - Some lenders offer more unusual loan products that might accept lower scores. These often come in the form of Adjustable-Rate Mortgages (ARMs) or loans with higher interest rates. These can introduce new and, in many cases, more significant risks.
- **Better Credit, Better Terms** - If your credit score is well above 620, you're likely to secure more favorable interest rates. It might be worthwhile investing time and resources into improving your credit.

- **Refinance vs. Purchase Rates** - Keep in mind that interest rates for refinances are typically higher than those for initial purchases. Be sure to factor those into your calculations.

Now, let's look at some less common scenarios:

- **Creative Lending** - Some investors find success with lenders who offer more flexible terms. These might be local credit unions or private lenders who are willing to look beyond just your credit score.
- **All-Cash Purchase** - If you're buying with cash, your credit score becomes less relevant. However, you'll still need to consider your credit for the eventual refinance.

Remember, lending requirements are always changing. What's true today might not be true tomorrow. Always check with local lenders for the most up-to-date requirements.

Skills Required

Here are the primary skills required for BRRRR:

- **Deal Analysis** - You'll need to evaluate properties not just for their current value, but for their cash flow potential after renovation.
- **Rehab Estimating** - Accurately estimating renovation costs is crucial. You'll need to develop a good understanding of construction costs, timelines, and potential issues that may arise during renovations.
- **Finding Discounted Deals that Also Cash Flow** - This is the foundation of successful BRRRR investing. You'll need to develop a keen eye for undervalued

properties that have potential as rentals after renovation.

- **Acquisition and Refi Financing** - Understanding various financing options is key. You'll need to be familiar with hard money loans, conventional mortgages, and refinancing processes.
- **Rehab and/or Rehab Management** - This skill can vary depending on your approach:

  - o **Self-Managing** - You'll need hands-on construction skills.
  - o **Managing Contractors** - This requires project management skills and the ability to effectively communicate with tradespeople.
  - o **Managing a General Contractor** - You'll need to understand the renovation process to effectively oversee the General Contractor who is managing the project.

- **Property Management** - Your approach here can also vary:

  - o **Self-Managing** - You'll need to understand tenant laws, maintenance, and financial management.
  - o **Hiring a Property Management Company** - This requires the ability to select and oversee a reliable company.
  - o **Short-Term Rentals** - This involves understanding platforms like Airbnb, as well as local regulations and hospitality skills.

Stability

Shane Parrish is a thought leader known for exploring mental models and decision-making strategies. His concept of active versus passive stability examines how systems maintain stability—either actively, requiring constant input and adjustment, or passively, maintaining themselves without intervention. This idea is especially relevant to the BRRRR strategy in real estate investing, as it raises questions about how stable your investment remains and what level of active management is needed to sustain it.

- **BRRRR is Very Actively Stable** - This means you'll need to be hands-on, especially during the initial stages. You're not just buying a property; you're actively improving it, finding tenants, and navigating the refinancing process.
- **Real Estate Investing is Generally Actively Stable** - Most real estate investments require ongoing attention. However, BRRRR takes this up a notch, particularly in its early phases.
- **Short-Term Rentals are Even More Active** - If you thought BRRRR was hands-on, short-term rentals dial it up further. You're dealing with frequent tenant turnover and constant property management.

Remember, while BRRRR starts off very actively stable, it can become more passive over time. Once you've refinanced and have long-term tenants in place, your day-to-day involvement typically decreases.

Scalability

When it comes to scaling your real estate portfolio, BRRRR offers a unique set of advantages and challenges compared to other strategies.

Let's dive into how BRRRR stacks up in terms of scalability:

- **Capital Efficiency** - BRRRR allows you to acquire properties with minimal money left in the deal. You might only leave 5% to 10% of the property's value invested, compared to 20% or more with traditional buy and hold. This means you can potentially acquire more properties with the same amount of capital.
- **Deal Flow Limitations** - Finding properties that meet BRRRR criteria can be challenging. You need deals that are discounted, can be improved, are in desirable areas for long-term holds and will cash flow as rentals. This often results in slower acquisition speed compared to other strategies.
- **Time and Effort** - BRRRR requires significant hands-on work, especially during the rehab phase. This time investment can limit how quickly you can scale your portfolio, as you'll be actively involved in each project.
- **Cash Flow Considerations** - Properties acquired through BRRRR may not cash flow as well as those chosen purely for their rental potential. This could affect your ability to secure financing for future deals, potentially slowing your scaling efforts.
- **Financing Flexibility** - BRRRR allows you to recycle your capital through refinancing, potentially freeing up

funds for your next deal. However, you'll need to navigate two rounds of financing for each property, which can be time-consuming and eat into some of your equity.

- **Market Dependence** - The scalability of BRRRR can vary greatly depending on your local real estate market. In some areas, finding suitable properties might be easier, allowing for faster scaling.

Risk Exposure

Let's dive into the risks associated with the BRRRR strategy. While it can be a powerful method for building your real estate portfolio, it's crucial to understand and prepare for the potential pitfalls. Here's what you need to know:

- **High Overall Risk Rating** - BRRRR comes with a significant risk profile due to its double risk exposure: you're facing risks during the rehab phase and then again as a long-term rental property owner.
- **Amplified Returns** - The use of leverage in BRRRR can magnify both your gains and losses. While this can lead to impressive returns, it also means you have amplified losses if things don't go as planned.
- **Negative Cash Flow Risk** - You might face an increased likelihood of negative cash flow, especially in the early stages. This is often due to:

  o Small or no down payments, which lead to higher mortgage payments
  o Limited selection of ideal cash-flowing properties, as you're often prioritizing properties that you can buy

at a discount and leave little in the deal versus optimal cash flow properties
- ○ Slightly worse financing terms, including higher interest rates, which can eat into your cash flow

- **Rehab Risks** - Renovation projects can be unpredictable. You might uncover unexpected issues, face contractor delays, or encounter budget overruns that could significantly impact your profitability.
- **Interest Rate Risk** - If interest rates rise while you're in the middle of a rehab, you could face higher costs when it's time to refinance, potentially affecting your ability to pull out your initial investment.
- **Market Volatility** - There's always a risk of property values declining during your ownership. This could impact your ability to refinance and pull out your initial investment, potentially leaving you with more money tied up in the deal than anticipated.
- **Rent Fluctuations** - If rental rates in your area decline, it could affect your cash flow and potentially your ability to cover your mortgage and other expenses.
- **Credit Risk** - Your credit score could be impacted if things don't go as planned, especially if you're leveraging multiple properties. This could affect your ability to secure financing for future deals.
- **Property Management Challenges** - Like any rental property, you'll face the usual risks associated with tenants and property management, including potential damage to the property, non-payment of rent, or high turnover rates.

Profit Speed

When it comes to real estate investing, especially with the BRRRR strategy, understanding the different areas of return is important.

Let's break it down into four primary areas and one secondary area.

The Four Primary Areas of Return

- **Appreciation** - This is the increase in your property's value over time. With BRRRR, you get two types:

  - **Natural or Organic Appreciation** - The gradual increase in property value due to market forces.
  - **Forced Appreciation** - The value you add through renovations and improvements. In BRRRR, this is where you can see significant gains by buying at a discount and rehabbing.

- **Cash Flow** - This is the money left over after all expenses are paid. Your cash flow timeline with BRRRR might look like this:

  - **Initial Rehab Period** - You likely won't see positive cash flow during this time. In fact, with a hard money loan at a very high interest rate, it is likely to be negative.
  - **After Rehab and Tenant Placement** - You should start seeing positive cash flow, typically right after rehab and tenant placement. Some rehabs and investors are faster than others, but it is not uncommon to see rental income within 3 to 6 months. However, with the higher interest rate loans while you're awaiting refinancing you might still be seeing negative cash flow for 6 to 12 months. Remember, rents and security deposits are usually paid in advance (rent usually at the beginning of the month of the rental period), giving you a very slight early boost.

- **Debt Paydown** - This is the portion of your mortgage that gets paid off over time. With BRRRR, your tenants are essentially paying down your mortgage for you. Often hard money loans for the rehab period are interest-only and do not have any debt paydown. You'll typically start seeing debt paydown after the refinance into long-term financing.
- **Tax Benefits** - Real estate offers various tax advantages, including depreciation. *Cash Flow from*

Depreciation™ can provide savings with each paycheck or at year-end, depending on how you structure it.

Don't forget about the money you set aside as reserves. You typically earn a return on the money while it is waiting to be utilized.

Speed and Size of Returns in BRRRR

Here's a breakdown of how quickly you might see returns and their potential size:

- **Appreciation -** You typically won't be able to access returns from appreciation until you sell or do a cash out refinance on the property.

  o **Forced Appreciation** - This can be substantial and quick. You might see a significant "paper" return as soon as your rehab is complete.
  o **Organic Appreciation** - This is the tendency for property values to increase over time from things inflation, and supply and demand. You typically see this accumulate slowly over time.

- **Cash Flow** - Rental income often starts as soon as rehab is complete and tenants occupy the property, but that's not the same as positive cash flow. With hard money loans on the property until you can refinance, you often won't see positive cash flow until after the property is refinancing into lower interest rate, long-term financing. That means positive cash flow might typically starts with the long-term financing after seasoning in 6-12 months.

- **Debt Paydown** - Equity from paying down the debt on the property builds slowly but steadily over time. Debt paydown usually starts once you refinance since many hard money loans are interest-only. Like appreciation, this is not easily accessed until you sell or refinance the property.
- **Tax Benefits** – Depreciation benefits and the resulting *Cash Flow from Depreciation*™ usually start as soon as you start renting the property.

Finding Deals

Let's look at the most common ways to find BRRRR deals and some of the more unusual, less common methods of finding BRRRR deals.

Most Common Methods

Here are the primary methods you'll want to focus on:

- **Multiple Listing Service (MLS)** - This is often your first stop. The MLS is a goldmine of information, but you'll need to dig deep to find a property in a desirable area you'll want to hold in that you can both buy at a discount and that will cash flow well once you've fixed it up and refinanced it.
- **For Sale By Owner (FSBO)** - These are sellers not represented by a real estate agent and not marketing their property in the MLS. They come in two flavors:

- o **Actively Marketed** - These are sellers that are actively marketing their property for sale (without a real estate agent).
- o **Hidden** - These are sellers that would consider selling but have not started to market their properties for sale.

  - **Marketing** - You may need to put out marketing to find these hidden sellers.
  - **Networking** - Or, find hidden sellers by networking and letting folks know you're interested in buying properties.

- **Wholesalers** - Build relationships with local wholesalers. They often have access to off-market properties that could be perfect for BRRRR.

More Unusual Methods

Let's dive into some unusual strategies that might just lead you to your next great BRRRR investment:

- **Auctions** - You'll find properties at foreclosure auctions, IRS auctions, and even local government auctions. Be prepared to act fast and have your finances in order, as these often require quick decisions and cash purchases.
- **Real Estate Owned (REOs)** - These are properties that banks have foreclosed on and now own. They're often eager to sell, which can translate to good deals for you. Build relationships with local banks and regularly check their REO listings.

- **Tax Lien/Tax Deed/Tax Sales** - When property owners fail to pay their taxes, local governments may auction off tax liens or the properties themselves. This can be a way to acquire properties at steep discounts, but it requires thorough research and understanding of the process in your area.

Remember, these strategies often require more legwork and due diligence than traditional methods. However, they can lead to unique opportunities that align perfectly with your BRRRR strategy.

Searching for Fixer Upper Deals

When you're hunting for BRRRR opportunities in the Multiple Listing Service, you're on a quest for the real estate equivalent of a diamond in the rough. You're not just looking for any old property; you're searching for a very specific combination of factors that can make your BRRRR property profitable in the short-term and long-term.

You're essentially looking for two crucial elements:

- **A Deeply Discounted Property** - This is a place you can buy for a discount, fix up, and then refinance to pull out as much of your initial investment as possible.
- **A Potentially Great Rental** - After you've rehabbed it, this property needs to generate solid cash flow as a rental in an area that you want to hold in for your desired holding period (usually long-term).

Finding a property that ticks both these boxes can be challenging.

Many investors, in their eagerness to get started, might let the second criteria slip.

You might hear them say, "If I can get a deal with nothing down, I'll make it work as a rental somehow." But remember, cash flow is important too even with the BRRRR strategy.

MLS Search Strategies

To uncover BRRRR opportunities in the MLS, you'll want to get creative with your search terms.

Here are some keywords to include in your searches:

- **Fixer-Upper Terms** - Look for terms like "handyman special," "fixer," "TLC," or "needs work." These often indicate properties that could be bought at a discount.
- **Problem Indicators** - Search for "mold," "asbestos," "damage," "fire," "smoke," or "water damage." While these issues can be serious, they often scare away less experienced buyers, potentially leaving opportunities for you.

Remember, these keywords are just the starting point.

You'll need to dig deeper to ensure the property meets both your discount and rental potential criteria.

Analyzing Deals

When analyzing the rental portion of your BRRRR deal, *The World's Greatest Real Estate Deal Analysis Spreadsheet*™ is an invaluable tool. This powerful spreadsheet helps you calculate crucial metrics like cash flow, return on investment, and long-term profitability.

Here's how you can use it effectively:

- **Input Property Details** - Enter the purchase price, expected rent, and estimated expenses to get a clear picture of your potential returns.
- **Analyze Cash Flow** - The spreadsheet automatically calculates your monthly and annual cash flow, helping you determine if the property meets your investment criteria.
- **Evaluate Long-Term Performance** - Explore how your investment might perform over time, factoring in appreciation and mortgage paydown.

- **Compare Scenarios** - Use the spreadsheet to compare different financing options or rental strategies to optimize your investment.

Remember, while this tool is excellent for analyzing the rental aspect, you'll need to separately assess the rehabilitation costs and potential after-repair value for a complete BRRRR analysis.

Download your free copy of *The World's Greatest Real Estate Deal Analysis Spreadsheet*™ at:

https://REFP.com/spreadsheet

Use it to analyze your BRRRR properties or any other rental properties you have.

Market Conditions

Some real estate markets are better for BRRRR than others.

Ideal

Here are the key characteristics of an ideal market:

- **Discounted Properties** - Seek markets where you can snag properties that need work at below-market prices. This gives you the opportunity to add value and boost your equity.
- **Strong Cash Flow Potential** - Look for areas where rental income comfortably covers your expenses. This ensures your investment generates positive cash flow from the start.

- **Appreciation Potential** - Target markets with a history of property value increases and promising future growth. This helps build your long-term wealth through appreciation.

If you're considering BRRRR for short-term rentals, don't forget to evaluate the short-term rental viability as well.

Challenging

What are challenging market conditions for BRRRR?

- **Negative Cash Flow Markets** - In some areas, even with a reasonable down payment, you might find yourself losing money each month.
- **Stagnant or Declining Markets** - Areas with no appreciation or, worse, negative appreciation can significantly impact the long-term viability of your BRRRR strategy.

Accessibility/Availability

Finding the perfect BRRRR property is like searching for a needle in a haystack. These deals are often elusive in the real estate market. Why? You're not just after any fixer-upper—you need a property that's ripe for renovation and has the potential to be a cash-flow powerhouse as a rental in an area that you want to hold in long-term.

Let's break down BRRRR property availability:

- **Market-Dependent Availability** - Some real estate markets are treasure troves for BRRRR opportunities, while others might leave you perpetually searching for a property that does not exist, like looking for an alligator in New York City. Alligators exist and you can certainly find them in some areas of the country, but trying to find one in New York City is very unlikely unless some family just released a pet alligator into the sewers recently.
- **Dual Criteria Challenge** - You're hunting for a property that ticks two crucial boxes: it needs work (to snag it at a discount) and must have strong rental potential in an area you want to hold long-term. This combo significantly narrows your options.
- **Expand Your Horizons** - Don't just stick to your backyard. Consider venturing into remote markets where BRRRR gems might be more abundant.

The beauty of BRRRR lies in its versatility. You can apply this strategy to a wide range of property types, from single-family homes to small multifamily properties like duplexes and fourplexes, and even commercial or industrial real estate. Plus, you have the flexibility to focus on traditional long-term rentals or pivot to short-term rentals for potentially higher returns.

But, finding a property that you can buy at a discount to add value and that would also make a good long-term rental in an area that you want to hold long-term can make them more difficult than either a fixer upper or rental individually.

Using Retirement Account

Self-directed retirement accounts can be utilized for BRRRR investing, offering a unique way to grow your retirement funds through real estate.

However, this approach comes with important considerations which making using them slightly disadvantages compared to non-retirement accounts:

- **Financing Changes** - When using retirement funds, you'll likely need to use non-recourse loans. These often require larger down payments and may have less favorable terms than traditional financing. This can hurt cash flow once you refinance due to the higher interest rates. Plus, these may also have variable rate loans interesting a new, additional risk to using more traditional, non-retirement accounts.
- **Work restrictions** - IRS regulations prohibit self-dealing. This means you cannot personally perform work on properties owned by your retirement account. All renovations must be carried out by third-party contractors. For some investors who are not doing the work themselves, this is a non-issue but if you plan to "save money" by doing work on the property yourself, this could be potentially problematic.
- **Lower refinance LTV** - Lenders may offer lower loan-to-value (LTV) ratios for properties held in retirement accounts during the refinance stage. This could limit how much equity you can access, potentially affecting the core BRRRR strategy. Or, it could require you to find

exceptional BRRRR deals that you're buying at even larger discounts to minimize the money left in the deal.

Using retirement accounts for BRRRR investing can be a powerful strategy, but it requires careful planning and understanding of the limitations.

BONUS CHAPTERS

Introduction to Real Estate Deal Analysis

Analyzing real estate deals can be a daunting task, but with the right tools and knowledge, it becomes much more manageable. One powerful tool we recommend is *The World's Greatest Real Estate Deal Analysis Spreadsheet*™. This spreadsheet is designed to help you evaluate the financial viability of real estate investments with ease and precision.

In our book, *How to Analyze Real Estate Deals*, we delve deep into the intricacies of deal analysis, providing step-by-step instructions and expert insights. This introduction aims to give you a high-level overview of the process and how to effectively use the spreadsheet to make informed investment decisions.

The spreadsheet allows you to input various data points such as purchase price, mortgage details, monthly income, and annual expenses. It then performs complex calculations to provide you with key metrics like cash flow, return on investment (ROI), and internal rate of return (IRR).

By leveraging this tool, you can:

- Quickly assess the profitability of potential deals.
- Compare multiple investment opportunities.
- Make data-driven decisions to maximize your returns.

Whether you're a seasoned investor or just starting out, understanding how to analyze real estate deals is crucial for success.

Download Spreadsheet for Free

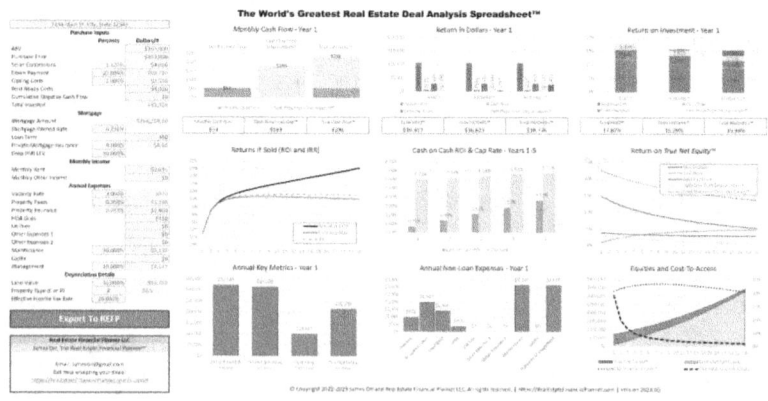

Unlock the full potential of your real estate investments by downloading *The World's Greatest Real Estate Deal Analysis Spreadsheet*™ for free.

Get your copy at: https://REFP.info/spreadsheet

We recommend always keeping an unedited, fresh copy on your hard drive in case you can't download the spreadsheet in the future.

Before analyzing a property, always make a new copy.

Spreadsheet Inputs

Entering the inputs into the spreadsheet is simple. Here's what you need to know:

- The manila fields indicate where you should input your data.
- The gray background with blue text shows the calculations that are automatically performed for you.

First, please name the deal that you're analyzing in the field just above the "Purchase Inputs". This will allow you to know which deal you're looking at if you're considering analyzing multiple deals or one deal multiple ways.

Purchase Inputs

Before we dive into the specifics of analyzing a real estate deal, let's go over the inputs required for the spreadsheet. These inputs will be divided into two columns: one for percentages and one for dollar amounts (or numbers).

Understanding what to enter in each field is crucial for accurately analyzing your deal. Let's go over what to put in each field next.

- **ARV** - Enter the After Repair Value, which is the estimated value of the property after all repairs and improvements have been made.
- **Purchase Price** - Enter the amount you are paying to acquire the property from the seller.
- **Seller Concessions** - Enter any financial concessions or incentives that the seller has agreed to provide, such as covering closing costs or offering repair credits.
- **Down Payment** - Enter the initial amount you will pay out-of-pocket towards the purchase of the property. Be sure to check out our guide on creative ways to come up with down payments for rental properties.
- **Closing Costs** - Enter the total costs associated with closing the real estate transaction, including title insurance, attorney fees, and other related expenses.
- **Rent Ready Costs** - Enter the expenses required to make the property ready for tenants, such as cleaning, repairs, and any necessary upgrades.
- **Cumulative Negative Cash Flow** - If you have negative cash flow enter the total cumulative amount of negative cash flow you anticipate before the property becomes cash flow positive. We recommend you set this aside to reduce risk. You may also want to check out our book on *How to Improve Cash Flow on Rental Properties* to get rid of negative cash flow on your properties.
- **Total Invested** - This is calculated for you. It is the cumulative amount of money you have invested in the

property, including **Down Payment, Closing Costs, Rent Ready Costs, Cumulative Negative Cash Flow,** minus any **Seller Concessions** you received from the seller.

Mortgage Inputs

To accurately analyze your real estate deal, it's essential to input detailed information about your mortgage and financing. These inputs will help calculate your monthly payments, interest costs, and overall financial commitment. Here's what you'll need to enter:

- **Mortgage Amount** - This is calculated for you. It is the total amount of money you are borrowing to finance the purchase of the property.
- **Mortgage Interest Rate** - Enter the annual interest rate for your mortgage. This is the percentage of the loan amount that you will pay as interest each year.
- **Loan Term** - Enter the duration of your mortgage loan in months. 360 months is a 30-year loan. This is the period over which you will repay the loan.
- **Private Mortgage Insurance** - Enter the monthly cost of private mortgage insurance (PMI) if applicable. PMI is typically required if your down payment is less than 20% of the purchase price. If you don't have PMI, use 0.000% here.
- **Drop PMI LTV** - Enter the loan-to-value (LTV) ratio at which PMI will be dropped. This is the point at which your equity in the property is high enough that PMI is no

longer required. If you don't have PMI, use 0.000% here.

Monthly Income

Accurately estimating your monthly income is critical for assessing the profitability of your real estate investment. This section will guide you through the necessary inputs for calculating your expected monthly income from the property, including rent and any additional sources of income.

- **Monthly Rent** - Enter the amount of rent you expect to receive from tenants each month. If you don't know how to determine what rent is on a property you're considering, you might want to check out our book on *How to Determine Rent Comps*.
- **Monthly Other Income** - Enter any additional monthly income from the property, such as parking fees, laundry services, or storage rentals.

Annual Expenses

Understanding and accurately estimating annual expenses is crucial for analyzing the financial viability of a real estate investment. This section will guide you through the various costs associated with owning and maintaining a property, from vacancy rates to property taxes and insurance. By thoroughly accounting for each of these expenses, you can better predict your investment's profitability and make more informed decisions.

- **Vacancy Rate** - Enter the percentage of time the property is expected to be vacant each year.
- **Property Taxes** - Enter the annual property tax amount you will pay for owning the property.
- **Property Insurance** - Enter the annual cost of insuring the property.
- **HOA Dues** - Enter the annual homeowner association fees, if applicable.
- **Utilities** - Enter the annual cost of utilities that you will pay as the property owner.
- **Other Expenses 1 and 2** - Enter any other annual expenses not covered in the previous categories.
- **Maintenance** - Enter the annual cost of maintaining the property, including repairs and routine upkeep.
- **CapEx** - Enter the annual amount set aside for capital expenditures. Consider our book and spreadsheet on CapEx for more guidance.
- **Management** - Enter the annual cost of property management services, if applicable.

Depreciation Details

Depreciation is a critical aspect of real estate investment analysis, as it allows you to account for the gradual reduction in the value of your property over time. Properly calculating and understanding depreciation can provide significant tax benefits and improve the overall financial picture of your investment. This section will guide you through the necessary inputs for determining depreciation, including land value, property type, and your effective income tax rate. By accurately inputting these details, you can optimize your investment strategy and maximize potential returns.

- **Land Value** - Enter the percent of the property that represents the value of the land. This value is used to calculate depreciation.
- **Property Type (C or R)** - Indicate whether the property is classified as commercial (C) or residential (R). This affects the depreciation schedule.
- **Effective Income Tax Rate** - Enter your effective income tax rate. This rate is used to estimate the tax benefits of depreciation.

Overrides

The spreadsheet is designed to be user-friendly on the Dashboard, while offering extensive functionality in the Overrides section. This dual approach ensures that users can easily navigate and input basic data, but also have access to more advanced features when needed.

In the Overrides tab, you have the ability to:

- **Modify any other inputs** - Adjust various parameters to suit your specific needs and scenarios.
- **Perform custom calculations** - Create and implement your own unique calculations to gain deeper insights into your investments.

- **View intermediate calculations** - Access detailed breakdowns of the calculations that drive the final results, providing transparency and better understanding.
- **Analyze performance over an extended period** - The spreadsheet allows you to conduct analysis through up to 40 years, enabling long-term strategic planning.
- **Track investment performance** - Use the Overrides tab to monitor how your investment evolves over time, making it easier to adjust your strategy as needed.

This comprehensive functionality ensures that the spreadsheet is not only a powerful tool for initial analysis but also a valuable resource for ongoing management and optimization of your real estate investments.

Dashboard

The Dashboard section provides a comprehensive overview of your real estate investment's key metrics and financial performance.

Here, you can quickly assess your monthly cash flow, return on investment (ROI), internal rate of return (IRR), and other critical indicators.

The Dashboard is designed to offer a user-friendly summary of your investment, allowing you to make informed decisions and track your progress over time.

Of course, you can dig into the Overrides tab for a ridiculous amount of additional detail.

Monthly Cash Flow - Year 1

This chart displays the Monthly Cash Flow, *Cash Flow from Depreciation*™, and the combined total, referred to as *True Cash Flow*™.

Understanding these metrics is crucial as they provide a comprehensive view of your investment's financial health.

- Monthly Cash Flow shows the actual cash inflow and outflow.
- *Cash Flow from Depreciation*™ accounts for tax benefits derived from property depreciation.
- *True Cash Flow*™ combines these figures, offering a more accurate representation of your investment's profitability.

Return in Dollars - Year 1

This chart displays the estimated dollars earned from your real estate investment over the first year, including Appreciation, Cash Flow, *Cash Flow from Depreciation*™, and Debt Paydown.

Understanding these metrics provides a holistic view of your investment's performance:

- **Appreciation** - Reflects the increase in property value over the year.
- **Cash Flow** - Shows the actual cash inflow and outflow.
- ***Cash Flow from Depreciation*™** - Accounts for tax benefits derived from property depreciation.

- **Debt Paydown** - Indicates the amount of principal paid down on your mortgage over the year.

Additionally, the chart includes earnings on reserves:

- **6 Months of Reserves in Savings** - Illustrates the interest earned if you set aside 6 months of reserves in a savings account.
- **Most of 12 Months of Reserves in Another Investment** - Shows the potential earnings if most of 12 months of reserves are invested in another investment vehicle like the stock market.

These combined figures provide a comprehensive representation of your investment's profitability and financial health over the first year.

You can see the totals at the bottom of the chart.

Return on Investment - Year 1

This chart displays the return on investment (ROI) from your real estate investment over the first year, including Appreciation, Cash Flow, *Cash Flow from Depreciation*™, and Debt Paydown.

Understanding these metrics provides a holistic view of your investment's performance:

- **Appreciation** - Reflects the increase in property value over the year divided by the total amount invested (and reserves where applicable).

- **Cash Flow** - Shows the actual cash inflow and outflow divided by the total amount invested (and reserves where applicable).
- ***Cash Flow from Depreciation***™ - Accounts for tax benefits derived from property depreciation divided by the total amount invested (and reserves where applicable).
- **Debt Paydown** - Indicates the amount of principal paid down on your mortgage over the year divided by the total amount invested (and reserves where applicable).

Additionally, the chart includes ROI on reserves:

- **6 Months of Reserves in Savings** - Illustrates the interest earned if you set aside 6 months of reserves in a savings account, divided by the total amount invested plus 6 months of reserves.
- **Most of 12 Months of Reserves in Another Investment** - Shows the potential earnings if most of 12 months of reserves are invested in another investment vehicle like the stock market, divided by the total amount invested plus 12 months of reserves.

These combined figures provide a comprehensive representation of your investment's profitability and financial health over the first year in terms of ROI.

You can see the totals at the bottom of the chart.

Returns if Sold (ROI and IRR)

This chart illustrates the return on investment if you sold the property each year for the first 20 years. It includes three key metrics:

- **Simple Annualized Return on Investment** - This metric shows the average annual return on your investment, calculated by dividing the total return by the number of years you held the property.
- **Compound Annualized Return on Investment** - This metric accounts for the compounding effect, showing the average annual return on your investment when considering the reinvestment of earnings.
- **Internal Rate of Return (IRR)** - This metric represents the annualized rate of return that makes the net present value (NPV) of all cash flows (both inflows and outflows) from the investment equal to zero.

These metrics provide a comprehensive view of the financial performance of your investment over time, helping you to understand the potential long-term profitability and compare it with other investment opportunities.

Cash on Cash ROI & Cap Rate - Years 1-5

This chart displays the Cash on Cash Return on Investment (ROI) and the Capitalization Rate (Cap Rate) for the property over the first 5 years.

Understanding these metrics provides a comprehensive view of your investment's performance:

- **Cash on Cash ROI** - This metric shows the annual return on your investment based on the actual cash invested. It is calculated by dividing the annual pre-tax cash flow by the total cash invested.
- **Cap Rate** - This metric represents the annual return on the property based on its current market value. It is calculated by dividing the net operating income (NOI) by the property's current market value.

By understanding these metrics, you can gauge the effectiveness and profitability of your investment, enabling you to make well-informed decisions and evaluate it against other potential investment opportunities.

Return on True Net Equity™

This chart shows you the returns you're earning from Appreciation, Cash Flow, *Cash Flow from Depreciation*™, and Debt Paydown divided by the equity minus the costs to access that equity with a sale (what we call True Net Equity™). It shows the first 20 years. It also shows the total of all four areas of return.

Understanding these metrics is crucial for assessing the true profitability of your real estate investment:

- **Appreciation** - Reflects the increase in property value over the year.
- **Cash Flow** - Shows the actual cash inflow and outflow.

- *Cash Flow from Depreciation*™ - Accounts for tax benefits derived from property depreciation.
- **Debt Paydown** - Indicates the amount of principal paid down on your mortgage over the year.

By dividing these returns by the True Net Equity™, you get a more accurate representation of your investment's performance, considering the costs to access the equity. This comprehensive view helps in making informed decisions and comparing the potential returns of different investments.

For more information on True Net Equity™ consider checking out our books about that:

- Should I Sell My Rental My Rental Property?
- Should I Sell My Refinance My Rental Property?

Annual Key Metrics - Year 1

This chart displays the financial performance of your real estate investment in terms of Gross Potential Income (GPI), Gross Operating Income (GOI), Operating Expenses (OpEx), and Net Operating Income (NOI) for the first year.

Understanding these metrics provides a comprehensive view of your investment's revenue and profitability:

- **Gross Potential Income (GPI)** - This metric represents the total income the property could generate if it were fully rented and all units were occupied at market rent rates, without accounting for any vacancies or losses.

- **Gross Operating Income (GOI)** - This metric reflects the actual income received from the property, including rent and other income sources, after accounting for vacancies and any collection losses.
- **Operating Expenses (OpEx)** - These are the costs associated with maintaining and managing the property, excluding mortgage payments and capital expenditures.
- **Net Operating Income (NOI)** - This metric is calculated by subtracting the operating expenses from the Gross Operating Income. It represents the income generated by the property after all operating expenses have been deducted.

By understanding these metrics, you can better assess the financial health and profitability of your real estate investment, helping you make more strategic decisions and compare it with other investment opportunities.

Annual Non-Loan Expenses - Year 1

This chart displays the financial performance of your real estate investment by itemizing all the non-loan expenses for the first year. Understanding these metrics provides a comprehensive view of your property's operational costs, which are crucial for accurate financial analysis and planning:

- **Vacancy Rate** - The percentage of time the property is expected to be vacant each year.
- **Property Taxes** - The annual amount paid for property taxes.

- **Property Insurance** - The cost of insuring the property for the year.
- **HOA Dues** - Annual homeowner association fees, if applicable.
- **Utilities** - The total annual cost of utilities paid by the property owner.
- **Other Expenses 1 and 2** - Any additional annual expenses not covered in the previous categories.
- **Maintenance** - The annual expense for maintaining the property, including routine repairs and upkeep.
- **CapEx** - The annual amount set aside for capital expenditures, such as major repairs or replacements.
- **Management Fees** - The cost of property management services, if utilized.

By breaking down these non-loan expenses, this chart helps you understand the total operational costs associated with your property, enabling you to better manage your investment and forecast its financial performance.

Equities and Cost-To-Access

This chart displays the equity in your real estate deal each year for the first 20 years, focusing on two key metrics: *True Net Equity*™ and Cash-Out Refi Equity.

- *__True Net Equity__*™ - This is the equity minus the costs to access it through a sale. It shows the real profit after considering selling costs.

- **Cash-Out Refi Equity** - This is the equity available if you refinance the property. It helps you understand the potential funds available through refinancing.
- **Cost-To-Access Equity Percentages** - The chart also shows the costs (as a percentage of the equity) associated with accessing each type of equity. This provides insight into the expenses involved.

Understanding these metrics is crucial for knowing how much money you could pull out of the investment over time and the cost to access that equity if you choose to do so.

Trademarks: The World's Greatest Real Estate Deal Analysis Spreadsheet™, Cash Flow from Depreciation™, True Cash Flow, True Net Equity™, and Nomad™ are trademarks of James Orr and/or Real Estate Financial Planner LLC. All rights reserved.

94 Ways to Improve Cash Flow on Rental Properties

You might find yourself in a real estate market where:

- Property prices are high—possibly even soaring,
- Mortgage interest rates are elevated—maybe significantly so,
- Yet rents, despite any increases, haven't risen enough to offset these higher prices and rates.

Instead of the steady stream of cash flow you anticipated, you may be seeing just a trickle.

As a real estate broker, I developed the *Lowest Monthly Payment Guarantee*™ for my clients. This comprehensive checklist—backed by a *cash-in-your-pocket guarantee*—promised to uncover every possible way to reduce and minimize their monthly payments when purchasing a property.

For my real estate investor clients, I went a step further and created the *Maximum Cash Flow Guarantee*™. This second checklist—also backed by a *cash-in-your-pocket guarantee*—was designed to help them identify every possible way to increase and maximize the income generated from their rental properties.

Simply put, cash flow is the difference between income and expenses.

By maximizing income and minimizing expenses on a rental property, you can significantly boost your cash flow.

Below, you'll find an abridged version of these two checklists—combined into one—designed to help you maximize cash flow on your rental properties.

For your convenience, I've organized the strategies into seven distinct stages of the real estate investing process.

7 Distinct Real Estate Investing Stages for Improving Cash Flow

The real estate investing process can be broken down into seven distinct stages, each offering unique opportunities to improve cash flow:

1. **Searching for Properties** - Strategies to enhance cash flow while you're searching for a property to buy.

2. **Financing the Property** - Tactics to maximize cash flow when securing financing for the property you're purchasing.

3. **Improving the Real Estate Investing Strategy** - Different real estate investing strategies produce varying levels of cash flow. Here, you'll find strategies tailored to the specific investing approach you choose once you've acquired the property.

4. **Improving the Property** - Cash flow enhancement strategies based on making physical improvements to the property itself.

5. **Marketing the Property for Rent** - Techniques to boost cash flow during the process of marketing your property to prospective tenants.

6. **While Owning the Property** - Strategies you can implement at any time during ownership to optimize cash flow.

7. **While Renting the Property** - Methods to improve cash flow while actively renting out the property.

While applying strategies from each stage will maximize your cash flow, you can also focus on the stage you're currently in. Implement what you can now, and revisit these strategies regularly to continuously improve—aim for just a 1% improvement each month.

Searching for Properties

Here are the cash flow improving strategies to implement while searching for a property to buy.

- **Agent Selection** - Choosing the right real estate agent can have a significant impact on your investment's cash flow. Some agents offer lower commissions or commission rebates. This money can appear as improved cash flow in the first year or use the money to buy down your mortgage interest rate and get improved cash flow for the life of the loan.
- **Lock/Float** - When securing financing for a property, interest rates can fluctuate. Locking in an interest rate early can protect you from rising rates during the closing process, while floating allows you to benefit from potential rate drops. This decision can directly influence your cash flow by affecting your monthly mortgage payments. This is especially important when buying properties that have extended under contract periods like when buying new construction.
- **Search for Less Expensive Properties** - Lower-priced properties often come with smaller mortgage payments, which can improve cash flow if you're able to get the same rent as their more expensive alternatives. For every $10,000 less expensive the property, you save approximately $50 per month (when mortgage rates are in the 5% range). Some lower priced prices will have commensurately lower rents. Analyze each deal carefully to ensure that the overall income and expenses align to boost your cash flow.
- **Search for Pretty Properties** - Consider purchasing properties that are already in good condition and don't require significant fix-up costs. By doing so, you can allocate funds that would have been used for repairs to

increase your down payment or buy down the interest rate, both of which can lead to better cash flow.

- **Search for Seller Concessions** - Seller concessions are contributions from the seller to help cover your closing costs. By negotiating for these concessions, you can reduce your out-of-pocket expenses or even use them to buy down your mortgage interest rate, both of which enhance cash flow. Consider searching for properties that are offering seller concessions.
- **Search for Creative Financing** - Creative financing can offer more favorable terms than traditional loans, directly impacting your cash flow. Here are several types of creative financing to consider:

  - **Search for Owner Financing** - Owner financing involves the seller acting as the lender, which can lead to better terms than a traditional bank loan. This can reduce your monthly payments and improve cash flow. We define owner financing as when the seller does not have a mortgage; if they have a mortgage that's wrap financing or buying the property subject to their existing mortgage which we will cover next.
  - **Search for Wrap Financing** - In wrap financing, you agree to pay the seller a monthly amount that "wraps" around their existing mortgage. The seller keeps their original mortgage in place and continues making payments to their lender. You, in turn, make payments to the seller that cover both the existing mortgage and any additional amount you've agreed upon. This can result in a lower overall interest rate compared to obtaining new financing, which can

improve your cash flow. Wrap financing also gives the seller the protection of foreclosure rights if you fail to make payments.

- **Search for Subject To**- In a "subject to" arrangement, you take ownership of the property while the seller's original mortgage stays in place. Instead of wrapping a new loan around the old one, you take over making payments directly to the lender on the seller's existing loan. The loan remains in the seller's name, but you're responsible for the payments. You're not formally accountable to the lender—it's not on your credit report—but you are responsible to the seller as per your agreement. This can be advantageous if the seller's mortgage has a lower interest rate than what's currently available. Like wrap financing, this can significantly reduce your mortgage expenses and boost cash flow. However, "subject to" financing typically doesn't offer the seller the same foreclosure protections as wrap financing does.

- **Search for Assumable Loans** - Some loans can be formally transferred from the seller to the buyer, keeping the original interest rate intact. If the seller's loan has a lower interest rate, assuming the loan can significantly boost your cash flow. Since most loan assumptions are for owner-occupant borrowers this strategy likely only applies to those utilizing an owner-occupant investing strategy like house hacking or Nomad™.

- **Search for Rent-To-Own Properties** - Rent-to-own agreements allow you to lease a property with the option to purchase it later. These arrangements can offer lower initial payments and more flexible terms, which may improve your cash flow compared to traditional financing.

- **Search for Agreements for Deed** - Also called bond for deed, contract for deed, or installment land contracts, these arrangements let you pay the seller directly over time. You get the deed after fulfilling the contract. This can lead to lower payments and improved cash flow while you're repaying.
- **Search for Seller Financing** - Seller financing typically involves the seller offering a loan to cover a portion of the purchase price, often as a second mortgage or "carryback" loan. In this scenario, you would secure the primary mortgage from a traditional lender, and the seller finances the remaining balance. For example, if you purchase a property for $200,000, you might get a $160,000 loan from a bank, with the seller providing a $40,000 loan. This setup can result in more favorable terms, such as lower interest rates or flexible payment schedules, improving your overall cash flow. Unlike owner financing, where the seller finances the entire purchase, seller financing usually complements other financing sources, reducing the need for a larger bank loan.

Once you've found a promising property using the strategies above, the next step is to optimize your financing to further enhance your cash flow. Let's explore the various ways you can improve your cash flow during the financing stage of your real estate investment.

Financing the Property

Here are the cash flow improving strategies to implement while financing the property you're buying.

Before Getting Loan

Here are a few strategies to improve cash flow to use before getting your loan.

- **Lender Selection** - Shop around for lenders to find one that offers better interest rates, lower fees, or more favorable terms. Different lenders have varying costs and requirements, so comparing multiple options on the same day can ensure you get the best deal, improving your overall cash flow.
- **Select by Closing Costs** - Some loans come with higher closing costs than others. By selecting a loan with lower closing costs, especially if you plan to finance these costs, you can reduce the amount you need to borrow, leading to better cash flow due to lower monthly payments.
- **Lock/Float** - Decide whether to lock in your interest rate early to protect against potential rate increases before closing, or to float and take advantage of possible rate decreases. Locking your rate provides security, while floating offers flexibility, both of which can impact your cash flow depending on market conditions.

- **Offer Less** - Negotiating a lower purchase price directly reduces the amount you need to finance, leading to lower monthly mortgage payments. This strategy can also leave more of your resources available for other cash flow improvement tactics.

Pay Upfront Instead of Financing

Here are some strategies for improving cash flow that deal with opting to pay fees upfront instead of financing them.

- **Seller Concessions** - Negotiate for the seller to cover some of your closing costs or to provide credits that can be used to buy down your mortgage interest rate. This is almost certainly required to be done at the time you make your offer and not after your offer is accepted. This reduces your upfront cash outlay and can lower your monthly mortgage payments, thereby improving cash flow.
- **Pay Closing Costs** - Paying your closing costs upfront instead of rolling them into your mortgage can reduce the amount you borrow, lowering your monthly payments and improving cash flow over the life of the loan.
- **Pre-Pay PMI** - If you're required to pay Private Mortgage Insurance (PMI), consider pre-paying it in a lump sum rather than monthly. This reduces your ongoing monthly expenses, leading to better cash flow.
- **Staggered Rate** - Opt for a staggered interest rate loan, where the interest rate is lower in the initial years

and increases over time. This can provide you with better cash flow during the early years of the loan when you may need it most.

- **Buy Down Rate** - Pay upfront to lower your mortgage interest rate for the life of the loan. A lower interest rate means a lower monthly payment, which can significantly improve your cash flow over time. For long-term buy and hold real estate investors—especially if you find yourself in a low mortgage interest rate environment—this can be an amazing strategy.

Change/Improve Borrower(s)

These strategies for improving cash flow relate to changing or improving the borrower on the loan.

- **Credit Score** - Improving your credit score can help you secure a lower interest rate and reduce your PMI rate. Both of these improvements lead to lower monthly payments and better cash flow.
- **Add Borrower** - Adding a co-borrower with a strong credit profile to your loan can help you qualify for a better interest rate and lower PMI, both of which can enhance your cash flow.
- **Remove Borrower** - If one borrower has a weaker credit profile, removing them from the loan might result in a better interest rate. This can lead to lower monthly payments and improved cash flow.
- **Loan Partner** - Partnering with someone who has a strong financial profile can help you secure better loan

terms, including lower interest rates and more favorable conditions, which ultimately enhance your cash flow.

Relationship With Lender

These cash flow improving strategies are based on your relationship with the lender or lending institution.

- **Auto Pay Loan** - Setting up automatic payments can sometimes qualify you for a slight reduction in your interest rate, directly improving your cash flow by lowering your monthly mortgage payment. It may show up also as a penalty to the interest rate if you don't use autopay for the mortgage.
- **Additional Accounts** - Maintaining additional accounts or depositing more funds with your lender might earn you a small interest rate reduction, leading to improved cash flow through lower monthly payments. This is more common with commercial loans and relationship banking.

Change Amortization

These strategies to improve your cash flow deal with changing the amortization schedule of the financing you're getting.

- **Interest Only** - An interest-only loan allows you to pay only the interest for a certain period, which significantly reduces your monthly payments. This can boost your cash flow in the short term, though it comes with long-term risks since the principal remains unpaid. You'll need to have a solid plan to deal with the loan balance when the ballon payment date arrives.

- **Negative Amortization** - A negative amortizing loan allows you to pay less than the interest due, causing the loan balance to increase over time. This lowers your initial payments and improves short-term cash flow but increases your debt over time.
- **Rate from Loan Term** - Shortening the loan term (e.g., switching from a 30-year to a 15-year mortgage) can lower your interest rate. However, this typically increases your monthly payments, so it's more about long-term savings than immediate cash flow improvement.
- **Loan Term** - Extending the loan term (e.g., from 30 to 40 years) reduces the monthly payment amount, which can improve your cash flow. However, this means you'll pay more interest over the life of the loan.

Loan Terms

These cash flow improving strategies deal with the terms (details) of the loan itself.

- **Amount Borrowed** - Putting more money down reduces the amount you need to borrow, leading to lower monthly payments. This can improve your cash flow, though it also means tying up more capital in the property.

- **Loan-To-Value** - A lower loan-to-value (LTV) ratio, achieved by making a larger down payment, often results in a better interest rate. This lowers your monthly payments and improves cash flow. Not only can putting more down improve your LTV and give you a better interest rate, but it might also reduce your Private Mortgage Insurance (PMI) payment since that's part of the calculation for determining PMI amounts.
- **Adjustable Rate** - An adjustable-rate mortgage (ARM) typically starts with a lower interest rate than a fixed-rate mortgage. This can enhance your cash flow in the initial years, though the rate—and your payments—can increase later.

Private Mortgage Insurance (PMI)

These strategies to improve cash flow deal primarily with Private Mortgage Insurance (PMI).

What is PMI? The lender would prefer you put at least 20% down to finance a property. With 20% down they feel comfortable enough that if you don't pay as agreed they will be able to foreclose, sell the property and get all their money back after the expenses of foreclosure and sale.

You insist on putting less than 20% down.

They may reluctantly agree, but they may charge you a higher interest rate because it is a riskier loan to them. And, additionally, they may insist that you pay a third-party insurance company a fee that insures them in case you default and they're unable to foreclose and sell the property to recoup their entire investment. This third-party insurance company is Private Mortgage Insurance.

It is insurance you pay for to protect the lender in case you default on the loan.

- **Eliminate PMI** - If you can put down at least 20% of the purchase price, you can avoid PMI altogether, significantly reducing your monthly mortgage expenses and improving your cash flow.
- **Pre-Pay PMI** - Paying PMI in a lump sum upfront instead of monthly can reduce your ongoing costs, leading to better cash flow throughout the loan term.
- **Improve Credit** - Enhancing your credit score can help you secure a lower PMI rate or even eliminate PMI altogether if your LTV ratio improves, both of which contribute to better cash flow.
- **Add Borrowers** - Added a borrower to your loan typically reduces PMI and therefore improves cash flow.

Other Properties

These cash flow improving strategies rely on tapping into other properties you own.

Some of these strategies deal with making sure your cash flow is optimized for your entire portfolio (including these other properties) and not specifically to a new property you're buying.

- **Cash Out Refi to Buy/Refi** - Consider doing a cash-out refinance on another property to use the proceeds for purchasing or refinancing your current property. This can result in better overall financing terms and improved cash flow.
- **Cash Out Refi for Larger Down Payment** - If putting more down on your current property will secure a better interest rate or eliminate PMI, consider using funds from a cash-out refinance on another property. This can lower your monthly payments and improve cash flow.
- **Rate and Term Before Acquisition** - Before purchasing a new property, consider refinancing your existing properties to better terms. As you own more properties the complexity of refinancing increases significantly. Consider this a reminder to consider this before each new purchase and to make any changes to other properties now before you add a new property that further limits what you can do. This can also improve the overall cash flow on your portfolio and might also allow you to qualify for better financing on the new purchase.

Non-Traditional Financing

These are some non-traditional financing strategies for improving cash flow you might want to consider.

- **Pay Cash** - If you have sufficient funds, paying cash for a property eliminates the need for financing altogether, which maximizes cash flow by removing monthly mortgage payments.

- **Private Financing** - Secure a loan from family or friends (private lenders) who might offer more favorable terms than traditional banks. This can lead to lower monthly payments and improved cash flow.
- **Creative Financing** - Explore options like owner financing, wrap financing, agreement for deed, lease-options, or subject to, where the seller might offer better terms than traditional lenders. These strategies can lower your mortgage payments and enhance cash flow.
- **Assumable Loan** - If the seller's existing loan has a lower interest rate than current market rates, assuming their loan can be a great way to secure better financing terms, leading to improved cash flow. This is more likely for owner-occupant loans, so this is probably limited to owner-occupant investing strategies like house hacking or Nomad™.

While optimizing your financing is crucial for improving cash flow, it's equally important to consider how your chosen real estate investing strategy can impact your returns. Let's now explore various strategies that can enhance your cash flow by refining your overall investment approach.

Improving the Real Estate Investing Strategy

Here are the cash flow improving strategies based on improving the real estate investing strategy you're opting to utilize.

- **Term** - Adjusting the duration of your lease can significantly impact your cash flow. Shorter-term rentals, such as daily, weekly, or monthly leases, often command higher rents compared to yearly leases. However, shorter terms can also lead to increased expenses, including higher vacancy rates, more frequent marketing, and potentially higher management and maintenance costs. Offering different terms, such as furnished vs. unfurnished rentals, can also cater to various market segments, like vacation rentals or boarding houses, providing opportunities to maximize income.
- **Lease-Option** - Lease-option strategies, including variations like rent-to-own (like lease-purchases and lease-options), can dramatically improve cash flow, particularly in markets where buying is significantly more expensive than renting. These arrangements typically involve collecting a non-refundable purchase deposit/option fee, which can—mathematically—appear to add hundreds of dollars per month to your cash flow. Additionally, tenants in lease-option agreements often treat the property with more care, reducing maintenance, vacancy, and management costs. This

strategy is a form of our *Deal Alchemy*™, where you trade future appreciation returns for immediate cash flow.

- **Niche** - Specializing in a specific rental market can allow you to charge premium rents by catering to unique needs. For example, you might focus on corporate rentals, traveling nurses, or student housing. By understanding and addressing the specific requirements of your niche audience, such as providing furnished units for corporate rentals or flexible leases for students, you can add value that justifies higher rental rates. The key is to determine what additional services or amenities you can offer that will attract your target market and what premium you can reasonably charge for those services.

The following cash flow improving strategies are really just variations of house hacking where you're renting out part of the property you're living in for income and to improve cash flow. However, you could utilize these strategies even when you're not living in the property.

- **Roommates** - Renting out individual bedrooms in a single-family home, or additional units in a duplex, triplex, or fourplex, can significantly increase your cash flow. This is a common house hacking strategy where you live in one part of the property and rent out the rest. For example, you might rent out spare bedrooms in your own home or lease the other units in a multi-family property. This approach allows you to maximize the rental income from a single property by utilizing every available space.

- **Rent by Bed/Bedroom** - Some properties, particularly those near colleges or universities, may lend themselves well to renting by the bedroom or even by the bed. This strategy works particularly well with student housing, where multiple tenants share a single property. By renting out each bedroom or bed individually, you can often achieve a higher overall rent compared to leasing the entire property to a single tenant.
- **Rent by Parts** - Renting out different parts of a property, such as non-conforming units in a duplex, triplex, or fourplex, can be a lucrative strategy. It's essential to check local occupancy laws to ensure compliance. This strategy can also include more unconventional setups, such as renting out RV parking spaces, tiny homes, garages, or storage units on the property. These spaces don't have to be residential; they can be rented for commercial or recreational purposes, such as storage or use of shared community amenities like a pool or recreational center.

While optimizing your real estate investing strategy can significantly boost cash flow, another powerful approach is to enhance the property itself. By making strategic improvements and modifications to your rental property, you can potentially increase its value and appeal, leading to higher rental income and improved cash flow. Let's explore some effective strategies for improving cash flow through property enhancements.

Improving the Property

Here are the cash flow improving strategies based on making improvements to the property.

- **Subdivide** - Consider subdividing your property into multiple units to increase rental income. For example, you could rent the upstairs and downstairs separately, offering tenants more privacy while still sharing common areas like heating, cooling, mail, laundry, and possibly even the kitchen or living areas. This isn't the same as converting the property into a formal duplex or triplex; instead, it's more about creating a roommate-like situation with more separation. This setup allows you to comply with local roommate laws and zoning requirements while potentially charging higher rents, as tenants may feel like they have their own space.
- **Upgrade Property** - Enhancing your property's curb appeal and overall condition can justify charging higher rents. Improvements could include landscaping, painting, adding or improving shutters, lawn care, updating the mailbox, property address numbers, or exterior lighting. These upgrades can attract higher-paying tenants and increase the property's value. This approach is also common in value-add strategies or the BRRRR method, where the goal is to improve the property to increase its rent and overall profitability.
- **Solar** - Installing solar panels and including the cost of electricity in the base rent can make your property more attractive to tenants who value energy efficiency, potentially allowing you to charge higher rents.

However, you should be cautious about the legal implications of charging for utilities, as this can sometimes enter a gray area. It's advisable to consult with a local attorney to ensure compliance with utility billing regulations.

- **Furnished Rental** - Offering a furnished rental can significantly increase the rent you can charge, especially if you shift your strategy to short-term or medium-term rentals, such as vacation rentals, student rentals, or corporate housing. Furnished rentals appeal to tenants looking for convenience and are often willing to pay a premium for a move-in ready home.
- **Convert Property** - Converting a single-family property into a duplex, triplex, or fourplex can increase your rental income by creating multiple rental units within the same property. This approach is especially effective if the property is already somewhat set up for such a conversion. However, it may be cost-prohibitive or even impossible if significant structural changes are required or if zoning laws restrict such conversions. Always check with your city and county regarding zoning and licensing requirements before starting any conversion work, as this can also affect the types of loans you can secure and their terms, including the loan-to-value ratio.
- **Improvement Rent** - Charging extra rent for specific property improvements can help offset the cost of upgrades while increasing your overall rental income. For example, you might charge a tenant more for installing new carpet or a fence. While you may not be able to recoup the full cost of the improvement from a single tenant, some upgrades, like a fence, can justify

higher rents with future tenants as well, allowing you to gradually recover your investment and potentially earn a return. This strategy is particularly useful for items with a long lifespan, where the cost can be spread out over multiple tenancies.

While property improvements can significantly boost your rental income, the way you market your property can be equally important for maximizing cash flow. By implementing effective marketing strategies, you can attract high-quality tenants, reduce vacancy periods, and potentially command higher rents. Let's explore some key strategies for improving cash flow through smart marketing techniques.

Marketing the Property for Rent

Here are the cash flow improving strategies to implement while you're marketing your property for rent.

- **Optimize Marketing** - Effective marketing starts with high-quality materials. Ensure that you have professional-grade photos, a 3D tour, and a video to showcase your property. These elements can significantly enhance the appeal of your listing, attracting more potential tenants. Additionally, use online marketing as well as flyers and signs strategically around the neighborhood to increase visibility. Well-designed marketing materials make your property stand out and convey a sense of professionalism that can justify higher rent and reduce vacancy periods.

- **Maximize Exposure** - To attract the right tenants, it's crucial to advertise your property across all available platforms where tenants might be searching. This includes online rental websites, social media, and community bulletin boards. Physical advertising, such as yard signs and directional signs leading to the property, can also capture the attention of local renters. By maximizing exposure, you increase the chances of filling vacancies quickly and with quality tenants.

- **Sales Skills** - Mastering sales skills is essential for renting your property at the highest possible rate and minimizing vacancy. This includes both phone skills for initial inquiries and in-person salesmanship during property tours. Being persuasive and knowledgeable helps you connect with potential tenants, address their concerns, and highlight the property's best features, ultimately leading to faster lease agreements and better tenant retention.

- **Optimize Showings** - Preparing your property for showings is a key step in securing a lease. Ensure the property is well-lit, smells pleasant, and is clean, neat, and in good repair. First impressions matter, and a well-presented property can make the difference between a potential tenant choosing your property over another. Additionally, create a sense of scarcity by scheduling back-to-back showings and mentioning this when booking appointments. This strategy can create urgency and increase interest among prospective tenants.

While effective marketing strategies can help attract tenants and maximize rental income, it's equally important to focus on optimizing your property's financial performance during ownership. Let's explore various strategies you can implement to improve cash flow throughout your tenure as a property owner.

While Owning the Property

Here are the cash flow improving strategies to implement while you own the property.

Refi/Pay Off Loan

Managing your mortgage can be one of the most effective ways to improve cash flow and overall property profitability.

- **Refi to Extend Term** - If your loan is old enough, consider refinancing to extend the loan term. This can lower your monthly payments and—if interest rates have dropped and/or your loan-to-value has improved—potentially secure a better interest rate, improving your cash flow.
- **Refi to Improve Rate** - If interest rates have dropped since you first took out your mortgage, refinancing to a lower rate can reduce your monthly payments and save you money over the life of the loan.
- **Payoff Loan** - If you have the financial means, paying off your loan in its entirety can eliminate your mortgage payments, drastically improving your monthly cash flow and reducing financial stress.

Taxes

Property taxes are a significant expense for any property owner, and managing them effectively can save you money.

- **Correct Assessor** - Ensure that the county assessor has accurate information about your property's condition and characteristics. Correcting any inaccuracies can prevent overvaluation and keep your taxes in check.
- **Contest Tax Increases** - If your property taxes increase, consider contesting the increase. Successful challenges can lead to reduced tax bills and improved cash flow.
- **Vote** - Participate in local elections and vote on measures that affect property taxes. Being informed and voting appropriately can help control future tax increases.

Insurance

Insurance is essential for protecting your investment, but it's also an area where you can manage costs.

- **Shop Insurance Rates** - Regularly compare insurance rates from different providers to ensure you're getting the best deal. Competitive rates can lower your insurance costs without sacrificing coverage.
- **Insurance Coverage** - Review your property insurance policy to make sure you have the right level of coverage. Avoid overpaying for unnecessary coverage or underinsuring your property. It is not just about

minimizing this cost while sacrificing coverage; you must make sure you minimize cost while keeping a desirable level of coverage. Sacrificing coverage is short-sighted and might significantly hurt cash flow if you ever have a claim that is you opted not to cover.

- **Insured** - Adjust your insurance policy by adding or removing people as needed to optimize your rates. This can lead to lower premiums.
- **Insurance Deductible** - Consider raising your deductible to lower your insurance premium. Taking on more risk personally can reduce your monthly insurance costs. See comments about sacrificing coverage being short-sighted above.
- **Remove PMI** - Totally different type of insurance, but if your property's equity has increased sufficiently, you may be able to remove Private Mortgage Insurance (PMI). This can significantly reduce your monthly mortgage payment.

Making Payments

How you manage your payments can also impact your overall costs.

- **Discount for Autopay** - Sign up for autopay on utilities and other bills to avoid per-bill fees. Many service providers offer small discounts or waive fees for customers who enroll in autopay.
- **Discount for Early Payments** - Some service providers, such as HOA or insurance companies, offer

discounts for early payments. Paying these bills in advance can reduce your overall expenses.

Management

Whether you manage your property yourself or hire a professional, effective management is key to maintaining profitability.

- **Self-Manage** - If you choose to manage the property yourself, ensure you stay up to date with the latest laws, best practices, and compliance issues. Self-management can save on property management fees, but it often requires a significant time investment.
- **Professional Property Manager** - Shop around for a high-quality property manager who offers reasonable fees. A good property manager can maximize your rental income and minimize headaches.
- **Manage the Manager** - Even with a professional property manager, it's important to regularly review management statements for accuracy. Mistakes can happen, and catching them early can save you money.
- **Insist on Best Practices** - Ensure your property manager follows best practices, such as marketing your property early and raising rents with each lease renewal. This proactive approach can help maximize your rental income.

Maintenance

Regular maintenance is crucial for keeping your property in good condition and minimizing vacancies.

- **Maintain Property** - Regularly maintaining your property can reduce the time it spends vacant between tenants. A well-maintained property attracts tenants quickly and reduces downtime.
- **Quality Materials** - Using quality materials for maintenance and repairs may have a higher upfront cost, but it can lower the overall cost of maintenance over time by reducing the frequency of repairs and replacements.

Depreciation

Depreciation can provide significant tax benefits, and managing it strategically can enhance your investment returns.

- **Accelerate Depreciation** - Consider accelerating depreciation on your property to maximize tax benefits in the short term. This strategy can improve your cash flow by reducing your taxable income, but it should be used with careful planning to avoid potential future tax liabilities. This can be one of the larger improvements to your cash flow.

While the strategies for improving cash flow during property ownership are crucial, it's equally important to optimize your rental income while renting it. Let's explore various techniques you can implement to enhance your cash flow during the rental phase of your investment.

While Renting the Property

Here are the cash flow improving strategies to implement while you're renting the property.

Add Services

Offering additional services can increase rental income and enhance tenant satisfaction.

- **Additional Services** - Consider offering additional services such as high-speed internet, cable, or utilities for an extra fee. Tenants often value the convenience of bundled services, making this an effective way to boost your rental income. However, be sure to check local laws, as this practice may not be permitted in some areas.
- **DFY Services** - Offer done-for-you (DFY) services such as lawn care, snow removal, or house cleaning. These services can be billed as extras, appealing to tenants who prefer convenience and are willing to pay for it.

Charge Appropriately

Setting appropriate charges can maximize your rental income while offering flexibility to tenants.

- **Bill Back** - Implement bill-back strategies for utilities or HOA services, such as charging tenants for non-potable water or other shared resources. This helps to ensure that tenants are covering their fair share of costs, improving your net income.
- **Tier Rent by Credit Score** - Adjust rent based on the tenant's credit score, with higher rent for those with lower scores. This can also apply to security deposits, where tenants with better credit pay less upfront. Check with your attorney before implementing this strategy.
- **Pet Rent** - Charge additional rent for tenants with pets. Pet rent can help cover potential wear and tear caused by pets and increase your overall rental income.

Convenience Billing

Convenience billing options can make it easier for tenants to pay rent while potentially increasing your revenue.

- **Billing Frequency** - Offer more frequent billing options, such as weekly or biweekly payments, instead of the traditional monthly schedule. This can be attractive to tenants who prefer smaller, more manageable payments but can also produce more cash flow over the same period.
- **Autopay** - Here are conflicting ideas where both options may ultimately improve cash flow. Encourage tenants to enroll in autopay by offering a discount or, conversely, charge a fee for those who do not use autopay. Autopay

can reduce late payments and ensure consistent cash flow.

- **Discount On-Time Payment** - Provide a discount for tenants who pay their rent on time or early, incentivizing prompt payments and reducing the need for late payment penalties.
- **Term** - Adjust the term of rental agreements to fit different rental strategies. Consider offering daily, weekly, or short-term/vacation rentals, which can often command higher rents than traditional monthly leases.

Timing

Optimizing the timing of lease agreements and renewals can minimize vacancies and maximize rental income.

- **Notice** - Require a 60-90 day notice from tenants if they intend not to renew their lease. This provides you with ample time to market the property and secure a new tenant, reducing vacancy periods.
- **Start Early/Test Rent** - Begin marketing the property early, even before the current tenant moves out, and start with a higher rent to test the market. This strategy allows you to adjust pricing based on demand and secure the best possible rental rate.
- **Renew Peak Season** - Align lease renewal dates to end during peak rental seasons, such as spring or summer, when demand is higher. This increases the likelihood of filling the property quickly and possibly at a higher rent.

Miscellaneous

Implementing additional requirements can protect your property and reduce potential liabilities.

- **Renter's Insurance** - Require tenants to carry renter's insurance. This protects both you and the tenant in case of damage to the property or loss of personal belongings, reducing potential conflicts and liabilities.

Conclusion

This guide has explored 94 ways to improve cash flow on rental properties across seven distinct stages of your real estate investing process.

Each stage presents unique opportunities to boost your investment's financial performance, and the cumulative effect of applying these strategies can significantly increase your property's profitability.

By focusing on cash flow improvement at every stage, you can:

- Build a more resilient and profitable real estate portfolio
- Enhance property values—especially for properties where value is driven by the income they generate, such as commercial properties
- Strengthen your ability to secure favorable financing by improving loan-to-value (LTV) and debt service coverage ratios
- Optimize tax benefits

- Accelerate savings for larger down payments and quickly replenish reserves
- Increase tenant satisfaction by enhancing the tenant experience, improving retention rates, and reducing turnover costs

Remember, even small adjustments across multiple areas can compound into substantial gains in your overall returns and financial stability.

Make it a habit to regularly review and implement these strategies, tailoring them to fit your specific properties and market conditions.

With consistent effort and strategic application, you can transform your rental properties into powerful, cash-generating assets that support your long-term financial goals.

Introduction to Monte Carlo Analysis of Rental Properties

There's a problem with how we've been modeling our investments so far. It is not unique to us. Almost everyone does it wrong.

But, we're going to fix it now.

The issue is the assumptions we've been using and how the real world works.

For the analysis we've been doing with *The World's Greatest Real Estate Deal Analysis Spreadsheet*™ (TWGREDAS)—and any other real estate deal analysis spreadsheet—we've used static assumptions.

We might assume that property values are going up by 3% per year. Well, that's not truly a correct representation of reality.

Heck, with the overrides tab in TWGREDAS we may have said, they go up by 3% for the first 3 years and then only 2% thereafter. Better, but still not reality.

The truth is: we really don't know how much property values will go up as we hold the property. They could go up by 3%. They could go down by 3%. They could go up then down or down then up. Could be more or less than 3%. Might be 3.1% or 2.9%. Might be up or down 6% or 10%.

If we look back at history (and we do when we consider the risks of investing in real estate), we can see what property appreciation has done over the last 100 years.

Risk Matrix: Appreciation

Severity				
0	**1**	**2**	**3**	**4**
Increase	*Small Decline*	*Medium Decline*	*Large Decline*	*Catastrophic*

Likelihood	Increase	Small Decline	Medium Decline	Large Decline	Catastrophic
1	>10% Increase 7.7%			10-15% Decline 6.0%	>15% Decline 0.0%
2	5-10% Increase 15.0%		5-10% Decline 12.8%		
3	0-5% Increase 25.6%	0-5% Decline 34.6%			

So, to correctly model how our investment might perform, we should not use a static 3% per year—or whatever static number you believe to be true—for property appreciation.

Our crystal balls are broken. We can't accurately predict—exactly—what appreciation will be for our properties.

We can guess. Based on what has happened in the past they will average about 3% per year.

But they may:

- Increase in value by more than 10% for the year about 7.7% of the time
- Increase between 5% and 10% for the year about 15% of the time
- Increase between 0% and 5% for the year about 25.6% of the time
- Go down in value between 0% and 5% for the year about 34.6% of the time

- Go down in value between 5% and 10% for the year about 12.8% of the time
- Go down in value between 10% and 15% for the year about 6% of the time

These are based on what has happened over the last 100 years. Could the future be different? Absolutely.

But it is much more accurate than just assuming that they will be going up in value by 3% per year every year.

Not Just Property Appreciation

As you probably guessed, this isn't just an issue with property appreciation. It applies to other assumptions we have as well.

Here's a list of some of the more significant ones:

- **Property Appreciation Rate** - This is the one we've been talking about already. It is how much properties go up or down in value.
- **Rent Appreciation Rate** - This is how much rents increase or decrease with each lease renewal.
- **Inflation Rate** - Inflation reflects the overall increase in prices and the decrease in purchasing power over time. It impacts everything from the cost of goods and services to the value of money itself. In the context of your portfolio, inflation affects how much your money will be worth in the future, influencing the real returns on your investments. For instance, even if your rental

income and property values rise, high inflation could erode those gains in terms of actual purchasing power. A million dollars today isn't the same as a million dollars 50 years ago and it won't be the same as a million dollars 50 years from now.

- **Mortgage Interest Rates** - **Mortgage Interest Rates** - Mortgage rates fluctuate over time. The rate you secure for your current property purchase or refinance won't necessarily be the same for properties you buy in one, five, or more years from now.
- **Stock Market Rate of Return** - This is how much you're earning on money you have invested in the stock market. This also applies to other investments you might have like savings accounts, bonds, CDs, cryptocurrencies, etc.

If you really want to go to freaky town, you could also model this with changing tax rates, insurance rates, maintenance and capital expenses on the property.

Does This Even Matter?

Does this even matter and why should I care?

Let's start with a simple example of someone who invests in stocks. They don't even buy a home to live in; they rent instead.

They invest approximately 10% of their income in the stock market earning 8% per year.

Using static assumptions, we could calculate that they would be financially independent (FI) after about 53.25 years.

See **Error! Reference source not found.** at the end of the chapter. We moved the charts to the end of the chapter—instead of inline—so we could show you larger, readable versions of the charts.

But what if we used a reasonable range of values for the return from the stock market instead of always 8% every year?

We could use a range of values that better approximates what the stock markets has done historically—still averaging about 8% for this selection of stocks.

Instead of seeing a smooth line showing their journey toward financial independence as shown in Error! Reference source not found. at the end of the chapter.

We'd instead see a less smooth line representing how the stock market returns change each month like Error! Reference source not found..

And, if we ran it 10 times, you'd see that when they actually achieve financial independence (when the line crosses the horizontal dotted line) is a little different each time. See Error! Reference source not found..

If the stock market performs well, they're financially independent earlier. If the stock market does not perform as well, they end up being financially independent later.

If we ran this 1,000 times and summarized the results, we can see the range of when they're financially independent. See Error! Reference source not found..

Monte Carlo Modeling

This type of analysis is called Monte Carlo modeling.

Monte Carlo modeling is a statistical technique used to simulate multiple potential outcomes for an investment or financial scenario.

It works by:

- Running hundreds or thousands of simulations with varying input parameters
- Analyzing the range and probability of different outcomes
- Providing a more nuanced understanding of potential risks and returns

For real estate investing, Monte Carlo analysis involves varying input factors such as property appreciation rates, rent increases, mortgage interest rates, inflation, and market returns. This approach allows you to better assess the likelihood of achieving your financial goals and understand the potential risks associated with your investment strategies.

I like to call it *Alternate Universe Modeling*™ because we're consider how your investments might perform if you were living in alternate universes with different futures.

Back to our example with someone just investing in stocks.

In Error! Reference source not found. at the end of the chapter:

- The light blue band shows the full range of results from the very worst to the very best.
- The darker blue band in the middle shows you the middle 50% of all runs. Half of the time the results are this darker band.
- The dark link at the very center shows you the median value. Half the values are higher than this. Half the values are lower than this.

If we look at the median line we can see that half the time they're financially independent around 58 years. Half the time it is after 58 years.

It could have been as early as year 48. And, it could take longer than 60 years—when we stopped modeling for this example. In fact, only about 85% of the 1,000 runs we ran were financially independent 60 years from when they started.

We can summarize this is a different chart and show what percentage of the 1,000 runs were financially independent in each month. That's Error! Reference source not found..

By using a range of values for things like the stock market rate of return, we get a much more nuanced understanding of what is likely to happen.

What If They Became Homeowners Instead of Renting?

Our last example they were renting a property to live in and investing in stocks.

What if they bought on owner-occupant property with 5% down to live in and invested in stocks?

If we used static assumptions they would be financially independent about 15 and half years faster as shown in Error! Reference source not found. at the end of the chapter.

Part of what gets them to financial independence faster is that they end up paying off their owner-occupant property 30 years after they buy it. Without a mortgage payment the threshold for them being financially independent is a little lower.

There's a little more to this story, but I don't want to go off into the weeds here. The punchline is they achieve financial independence faster with static assumptions as you can see in Error! Reference source not found..

Let's vary the property appreciation rate, mortgage interest rate, inflation rate, and stock market rate of return. If we were discussing rentals, we'd vary the rent appreciation rate as well but in this case they're not buying any rentals; we'll get to that shortly.

With variable property appreciation rates, mortgage interest rates until they lock in a 30-year fixed rate financing loan, inflation rate and stock market rate of return it looks like Error! Reference source not found..

They're financially independent as early as 33.75 years from when they start. In 99.5% of the 1,000 runs they're financially independent by the time we stop modeling at 60 years.

How does this compare to them just investing in stocks? Let's show both on one chart in Error! Reference source not found..

Buying an owner-occupant property seems to make a pretty big difference.

If we just look at what percentage of the 1,000 runs they achieve financial independence, you can see that buying the owner-occupant property is more probable (higher percentage of the runs achieve it) and they're financially independent earlier (it happens more to the left on the chart). See Error! Reference source not found..

Buying Rental Properties with 20% Down Payments

Let's assume, for now, that they don't buy an owner-occupant property with 5% down. Instead, they decide to buy 20% down rental properties as their primary investing strategy.

Any additional money beyond what they need for the rentals is still investing in stocks, but whenever they get enough for a 20% down payment they buy a rental property with very modest cash flow.

They're willing to buy up to ten 20% down payment rentals.

If we have **static assumptions** for property appreciation, rent appreciation, inflation, mortgage interest rates and the stock market rate of return, they might be financially independent after 31 years.

With static assumptions, that's about 18.67 years faster than just investing in stocks and about 3 years faster than buying an owner-occupant property and investing stocks as shown in Error! Reference source not found..

With static assumptions, they achieve financial independence faster. See Error! Reference source not found..

And, still looking at the chart above, they appear have a lot more income coming then just investing in stocks the longer they hold the rental properties.

In fact, they're earning about twice what they need to be financially independent about 48.5 years in. That means they're earning twice what they need to be financially independent before just investing in stocks as a renter is even earning enough for them to financially independent at all.

Not long after they achieve financial independence just investing in stocks as a renter, they're earning 3 times what they need to be financially independent with their 10 rentals.

But, this is about Monte Carlo modeling, so what if we did vary property appreciation rates, rent appreciation rates, inflation, mortgage interest rates and the stock market rate of return?

It is important to realize that because the property prices vary with each run sometimes the properties they're buying can be slightly more or less expensive. On average though, property prices are going up at about 3% per year.

Rent is similar. Rents can go up or down, but overall, rents are increasing by about 3% per year.

Mortgage interest rates started at about 8.5% for a non-owner-occupant loan without paying significant points. But, mortgage interest rates can get better—or worse—over time as they're acquiring properties. That means sometimes properties will cash flow better and sometimes they'll cash flow a little worse.

Let's look at their journey to financial independence buying ten 20% down payment rentals in Error! Reference source not found..

You can see there are times when the market goes in their favor (both the real estate and stock market) they achieve financial independence early. And, there are times when they still don't quite achieve it through 60 years.

How does it compare to the two previous strategies: renting and investing exclusively in stocks and buying an owner-occupant property and exclusively investing in stocks? See Error! Reference source not found..

It is getting harder to see what is happening in the chart as we add additional comparisons.

We can make it easier in two different ways. First, we can look at the same chart, but turn off the shaded areas for each strategy.

This would leave just the median—or the middle-most result—where half of them are better and half are worse. That's Error! Reference source not found..

This chart doesn't show up the range of results (how early or late they achieve FI) but it does show how much more they're likely to earn by buying the rentals by what percent of their financial independence goal they're earning.

By earning a higher percentage of the amount they need to be financially independent, they're able to support a higher standard of living.

In other words, if they needed to be earning $10,000 per month passively to be considered financially independent, but their earning 200% of that—or $20,000 per month—they could live at a much higher standard of living on $20,000 per month than the $10,000 per month that they needed—at a minimum—to be considered financially independent.

The second way to make it easier to see what is happening is looking at the percentage of the 1,000 runs that achieved financial independence like we did previously. That's Error! Reference source not found..

Buying ten 20% down payment rentals sees them achieving financial independence earlier (more left on the chart above) and then has a similar success rate to what they'd see if they bought an owner-occupant and invested in stocks.

Owner-Occupant, Rentals and Stocks

I think you know what's coming next: what if they bought an owner-occupant property with 5% down, then bought up to nine more rental properties, each with 20% down payments and invested the rest in stocks?

With static assumptions that's about 3.5 years faster than just renting and buying ten 20% down payment rentals. See Error! Reference source not found..

If we do Monte Carlo modeling, it looks like Error! Reference source not found..

Doing a very busy version of this chart by comparing it to the other strategies so far, it looks like Error! Reference source not found..

If we just look at the 50th percentile (median) value for the four options as seen in Error! Reference source not found..

It shows that buying the owner-occupant property and nine 20% down payment rentals appears to be faster and gives them a higher standard of living than even buying ten 20% down payment rentals.

If we look at the percentage of the 1,000 runs for reach strategy that achieved financial independence and when, we can see that buying an owner-occupant property and then nine 20% down rentals is the best performer yet as seen in Error! Reference source not found..

In the chart above you can see that not only does financial independence tend to happen faster (a little to the left on the chart), it also tends to be more consistent (a higher percentage of the runs achieve FI).

Nomad™ Real Estate Investing Strategy Example

There's so much more we could do with this, but for now I'll wrap it up with a slight curve ball.

Instead of buying an owner-occupant property and then buying nine 20% down payment rentals, let's imagine they Nomad™.

- They buy an owner-occupant property with 5% down payment.
- They live there for *at least* a year. That's a requirement of the lender to get an owner-occupant loan with an owner-occupant down payment and owner-occupant mortgage interest rate.

- Once their year is up AND they've saved up enough for another 5% down payment, they buy another owner-occupant property and move into it.
- They take the previous property they were living in and convert it to a rental property
- They repeat this until they have 9 rentals and the property they're living in

Instead of having to save up for 20% down payments, they acquire the same nine rental properties with only 5% down on each by moving into each one as an owner-occupant.

Is this better? Is this more probable for them to be financially independent? Is this faster to financial independence? Does this give a higher standard of living than the other strategies so far? And—we won't cover it here because it is a longer discussion—but is it more or less risky?

It turns out that with static assumptions (not Monte Carlo modeling yet), Nomad™ is 58 months (almost 5 years) faster to financial independence. See Error! Reference source not found..

If we add variability and do Monte Carlo modeling, we can look at how the Nomad™ strategy performs in Error! Reference source not found..

Brace yourself for the busy version comparing them all at the same time in Error! Reference source not found..

And, if we turn off the range of results and just look at the middle most (median) of the 1,000 runs for each strategy, we can see the following in Error! Reference source not found..

Still a bit busy to see what is going on, but I will point out, in the chart above, the Nomad™ strategy seems to give them the fastest achievement of financial independence and highest standard of living.

Isn't it interesting.

If we look at the percentage of the 1,000 runs that achieve financial independence and by when you can see even better in Error! Reference source not found..

The Nomad™ strategy achieves financial independence earliest (to the left on the chart above). It also has a higher probability of being financially independent earlier.

Additional Modeling

Now that we know the importance of considering the variability that might occur in the future, this is really just the beginning.

There is a ridiculous amount more to dig into here. We've just barely scratched the surface.

There's a lot more to model.

For example, we could model each strategy you're considering seeing how each strategy performs:

- Buying long-term buy and hold rental properties (short-term rentals, medium-term rentals, student rentals, storage units, assisted living, apartments, etc)

- Buying properties utilizing creative financing (owner financing, wrap financing, loan assumptions, rent-to-owns, agreements for deed, subject-to)
- Variations on the Nomad™ strategy (Nomad™ by Proxy, Nomad™ with House Hacking, Nomad™ to Short-Term Rental, Nomad™ with Lease-Option Exits, *The Ultimate Real Estate Agent Retirement Plan™*)
- House Hacking and related strategies
- Short-Term Rentals and related strategies
- Flipping properties and related strategies
- BRRRR and related strategies
- And much, much more

Or, combining one or more of these strategies at the same time (fix and flipping while acquiring long-term or short-term rentals as an example) or sequentially (fix and flipping for 10 years then switch to buy and hold).

Or, we could test a wide assortment of variations to your strategy:

- More or less reserves (and its impact on both speed and risk)
- More or less down payment size up to buying properties for all cash
- Buying down interest rates or not
- Getting roommates or not (house hacking)
- Selling via lease-options versus with a real estate agent or for sale by owner
- Paying off properties early with extra cash flow versus not

- Doing cash out refinances to buy additional properties faster
- Buying properties and selling them when you could take the proceeds (after all expenses including taxes) and then investing that money in stocks, bonds or something else to be financially independent
- Buying more properties than you need and selling them to pay off properties when it means you'd be financially independent
- And much, much more

Not Just Financial Independence

When we do these models, it is important to consider more than just how fast you're able to get to financial independence—even though that's what we focused on here.

Sometimes it is about your standard of living once you are financially independent. Some strategies might just barely get you to your minimum required income to be financially independent. While others will give you far more each month than you initially stated you needed allowing you to live at a much higher standard of living than you originally required.

Sometimes, it is about measuring, comparing and ultimately minimizing risks. Some strategies are riskier than others. They might get you to financial independence, on average, 1 year faster, but there's a 20 times greater chance you'll run out of money by pursuing that strategy than another one that gets you to financial independence, on average, a year slower.

That all might be worth considering... especially for your own unique situation.

It is important for you to evaluate your own strategy utilizing Monte Carlo modeling to better understand how to achieve financial independence faster, easier, with higher probability of success, with a higher standard of living and with less overall risk.

Or, if you are going to ignore one or more of those things, deliberately and strategically choosing to ignore them with full knowledge of the consequences.

Figure 1

Figure 2

Figure 3

Figure 4

114

Figure 5

Figure 6

Figure 7

Figure 8

Figure 9

Figure 10

Figure 11

Figure 12

Figure 13

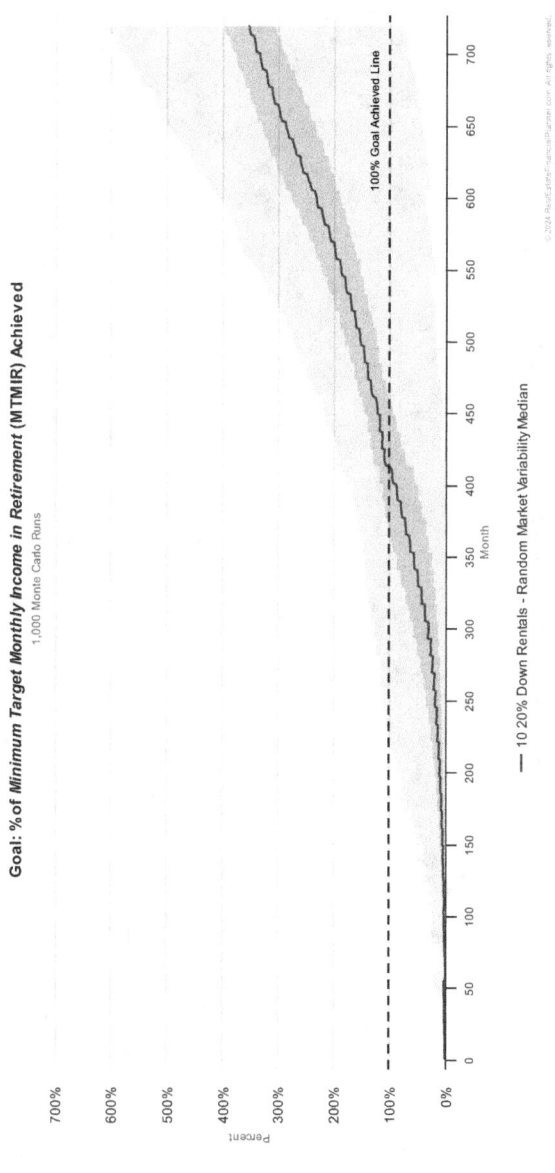

Goal: % of *Minimum Target Monthly Income in Retirement (MTMIR)* Achieved

1,000 Monte Carlo Runs

100% Goal Achieved Line

Month

Percent

700%
600%
500%
400%
300%
200%
100%
0%

— 10 20% Down Rentals - Random Market Variability Median

Figure 14

Figure 15

Figure 16

Figure 17

Figure 18

Figure 19

Figure 20

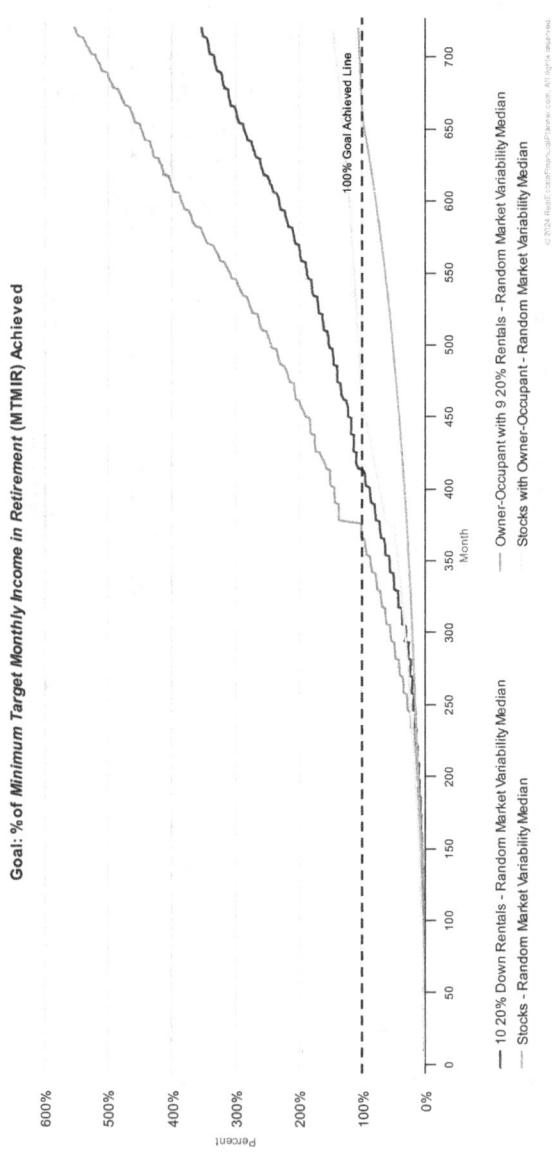

Goal: % of *Minimum Target Monthly Income in Retirement (MTMIR)* Achieved

Figure 21

Figure 22

Figure 23

Figure 24

Figure 25

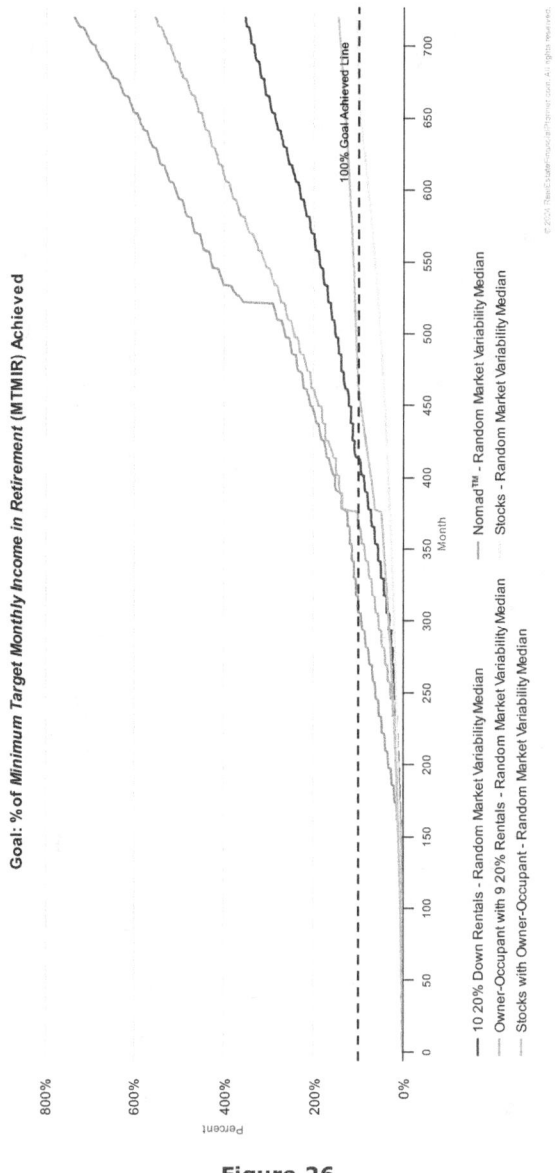

Goal: % of *Minimum Target Monthly Income in Retirement (MTMIR)* Achieved

Figure 26

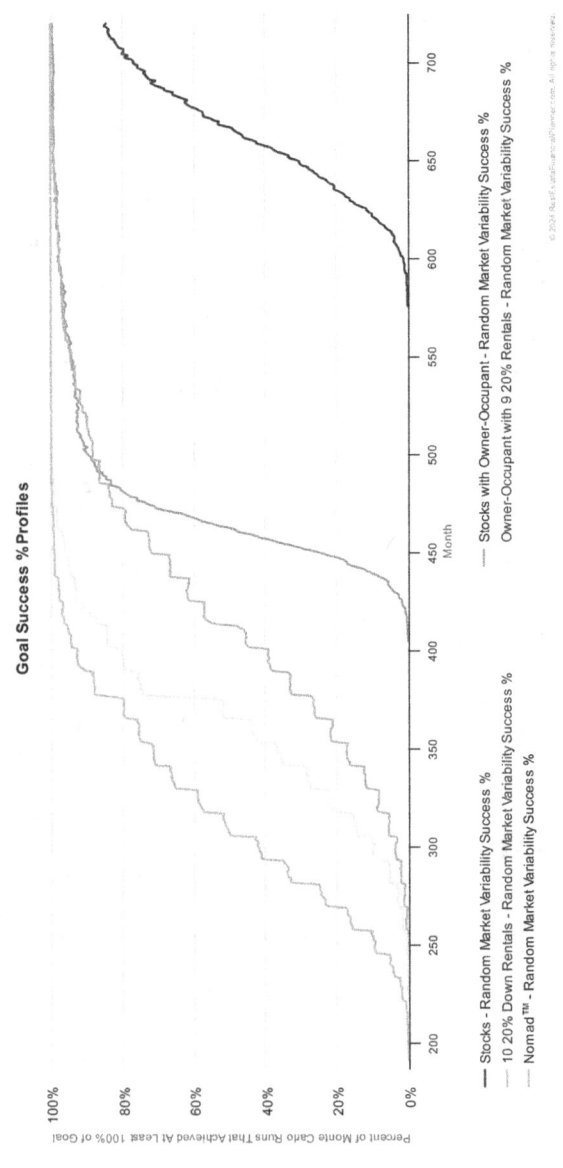

Figure 27

About the Author

James Orr is a seasoned real estate investor and the visionary creator of the Real Estate Financial Planner™ software. With a passion for sharing his wealth of knowledge, James has authored numerous books on real estate investing, covering a wide array of topics to help both novice and experienced investors succeed.

Living in Loveland, Colorado, James enjoys a fulfilling life with his wife, Tammy, whom he has been happily married to since 1995. Together, they have raised two grown sons. When he's not writing or managing his real estate investments, James is dedicated to teaching others the secrets of financial independence through smart property investments.

Also by James Orr

- The Real Estate Investing Mentor series of topic books
- How to Achieve Financial Independence and Live Your Passion Regardless of Age or Income: 10 Paths to Financial Independence Analyzed
- How to Acquire a Multi-Million Dollar Real Estate Portfolio With Just $3,000
- How to Acquire a Multi-Million Dollar Real Estate Portfolio Earning Just $5,000 Per Month
- Nomad™
- Ultimate Nomad™ Checklist
- Northern Colorado Real Estate Advisor
- Acquiring a Portfolio of Cash Flowing Properties In Northern Colorado: A Real Estate Financial Planner™ Blueprint
- Real Estate Investing Systems

Software and Spreadsheets

- Real Estate Financial Planner™ software
- The World's Greatest Real Estate Deal Analysis Spreadsheet™
- Should I Sell My Rental Property Spreadsheet™
- Should I Refinance My Rental Property Spreadsheet™
- CapEx Estimator for Rental Property – Basic and Advanced Spreadsheets
- Financial Independence Asset Allocation and Cash Flow Engines Spreadsheet™
- The Investor's Agent One-Page Business Plan™

A Small Request

Thank you for reading *The Real Estate Investing Mentor: The Affordable $50K Coaching Alternative* topic book on **Introduction to BRRRR Real Estate Investing**.

I am positive if you follow what I've written, you will be on your way to successfully investing in real estate. When you do please reach out and share your story.

I have a small, quick favor to ask. Would you mind taking a minute or two and leaving an honest review for this book on Amazon?

Reviews are the BEST way to help others purchase this book and keep the price of my books low for everyone, and I check all my reviews looking for helpful feedback.

Please visit:

https://REFP.info/intro-brrrr-book

Questions?

Thank you for taking the time to read this book. If a concept sparked a question or if you feel there's an area that could be explained more clearly, I'd truly appreciate hearing from you. You can reach me at **jamesorr@gmail.com** with any feedback specific to this title. My goal is to make each book as helpful and practical as possible, and your input plays a big part in that.

Just a note—while I'm here to help deepen your understanding of this book's topics, this isn't intended as a personal coaching service. For advice tailored to your own situation, I encourage you to work closely with a real estate agent who can provide the insight and support unique to your goals.

Thank you again for reading, and for helping me make this series an even better resource for investors like you.